Design Patterns

Christopher G. Lasater

Wordware Publishing, Inc.

Library of Congress Cataloging-in-Publication Data

Lasater, Christopher G.
   Design Patterns / by Christopher G. Lasater.
      p. cm.
   Includes index.
   ISBN-10: 1-59822-031-4 (pbk.)
   ISBN-13: 978-1-59822-031-5
   1. Software patterns. 2. Object-oriented programming (Computer
science). I. Title.

   QA76.76.P37L37 2006
   005.1--dc22   2006027625

© 2007, Wordware Publishing, Inc.

All Rights Reserved

1100 Summit Avenue, Suite 102
Plano, Texas 75074

No part of this book may be reproduced in any form or by
any means without permission in writing from
Wordware Publishing, Inc.

Printed in the United States of America

ISBN-10: 1-59822-031-4
ISBN-13: 978-1-59822-031-5
10 9 8 7 6 5 4 3 2 1
0609

All inquiries for volume purchases of this book should be addressed to Wordware
Publishing, Inc., at the above address. Telephone inquiries may be made by
calling:

(972) 423-0090

To Lorenzo and Lena. Without them I wouldn't have had the strength or courage to write this book.

Contents

Introduction

Design patterns have been around for quite a few years. They were originally created by the Gang of Four (Erich Gamma, Richard Helm, Ralph Johnson, and John Vlissides), which is responsible for formalizing the accepted design patterns we use today. Their use, while questioned and argued over by different programming schools of thought, has generally been accepted as "best practices" within the development community. The original takeoff of design patterns was brought about in the Java and C++ world.

Other languages like .NET (dot NET) have sprung up in recent years to fill certain marketing and technology voids left open by these languages, and have adopted design patterns in one way or another to mimic what was learned by programmers in Java and C++. Even the previously script-oriented syntax of Visual Basic has blossomed into a fully object-oriented language, via Visual Basic.NET. Microsoft also added a Java-like language, which has related syntax and framework structure, in the form of C#, which is so much like Java that applying design patterns is a relatively expected conjecture.

Most programmers new to object-oriented languages seem to have the same dilemma when faced with whether or not to use or learn design patterns: *Why should I?* Usually the problem is that the ability and time required for learning patterns-based programming is at a premium and the return seems dubious. Someone not familiar with the why behind the methodology certainly will not continue on to the what and where. So explaining to people new to the concept why they should spend the time learning design patterns can be difficult.

Another issue is availability and ease of dissemination of the relevant data. There have been numerous books and papers written on the uses and methodology of design patterns, but to a junior developer looking to improve basic skills or learn the skills needed to get a job, having to read complicated texts to learn a new methodology or way of thinking is out of the question. Senior developers looking to upgrade current skills can have similar issues, in that to augment their skill sets they have to do a large amount of research just to be able to understand the basics. Most of the texts available on design patterns are not easily referenced, and require an expanded understanding of object-oriented methodologies and patterns to even get through, and full comprehension may require reading the material several times from start to finish. There have been a few attempts to "dumb down" the data, but these seem to be more playful than useful, and leave project developers a little turned off by the lack of serious content of the work.

As a developer, as well as a development manager, I can assure you I have had the same problems. Whether learning to use patterns or teaching them to others, I found there was no quick and easy reference to explain or learn which pattern is appropriate in which case and why. I often struggled with the basics of object-oriented design when learning patterns, and had to learn the hard way which methods worked where. One thing I did find was that design patterns were created and have evolved from the work of everyday code practices, and many developers are using them without actually knowing the established 23 patterns. When I first started to pattern, I often had to search through many texts and websites, accessing several sources to understand a particular pattern. This was hard when trying to meet deadlines, since time was crucial, and the only reason I persisted in learning was because I saw there was a lot of value in what I did manage to understand.

After several years of this kind of thing, I began to write some articles for the Code Project site (www.codeproject.com). I started with aspects of things about which I saw value, but I thought were under-documented. I wrote in a fashion that I would like to read, something without a lot of complicated dialog that just stated problems and solutions in code and explanations of what I was doing and why. After a while I realized a lot of people seemed to respond to what I had written. That was when I decided that I should write this book.

Audience and Goal

The goal of this book is to give you, the reader, an easy to reference library of the recognized 23 design patterns as well as some principles of object-oriented programming that will help you become a better designer. I wrote this book for a specific audience, but I hope I wrote it in a way that those who are not coders can also get something out of it. The audience I am trying to reach is project developers, coders who do not have the time or patience for complicated or glitzy texts, but need real-world answers they can easily follow and use immediately in their own code.

Assumptions This Book Makes

I wrote the book exactly as I would like to read such a book; the descriptions are simple and easy to follow, there is little in the way of complicated theorems and scientific explanations of patterns, and the examples can be applied immediately to existing code bases. Having mentored hundreds of developers in the use of patterns and object-oriented design practices and having overseen many projects for major corporations, I have been able to compile a style of writing and teaching that enables a simple and practical approach to understanding patterns-based programming. As you read this book, you will notice that I do not go into details about the theoretical aspects of patterns, but instead speak directly to situational and logical implementations. This is not without purpose. I am assuming that the readers who will have interest in this book are looking for *practical* information, not theoretical. There are many such theoretical patterns texts available today that go into any depth you desire to expand on the theory behind patterns. That is not the aim of this book. This book is for people who are looking for practical implementations of patterns. I assume that the reader has a basic knowledge of code and object-oriented principles and syntax, but any in-depth knowledge is not needed. Any developer familiar with languages like Java, C++, C#, VB.NET, or Eiffel will be able to follow the example problems and solutions and easily transpose them into their functional code.

Conventions Used in This Book

The following typographical conventions are used in this book:

Plain text

> Indicates text body.

Italic

> Indicates emphasis and terms that are in the glossary.

`Constant width`

> Indicates the contents of files or the output from commands.

`Courier`

> Indicates commands, options, switches, variables, attributes, keys, functions, types, classes, namespaces, methods, modules, properties, parameters, values, objects, events, event handlers, XML tags, HTML tags, and macros.

Using Code Examples

This book is here to help you get your job done. In general, you may use the code in this book in your programs and documentation. (The example code can be downloaded from www.wordware.com/files/dp0314.) You do not need to contact us for permission unless you're reproducing a significant portion of the code. For example, writing a program that uses several chunks of code from this book does not require permission. Selling or distributing a CD-ROM of examples from this book does require permission. Answering a question by citing this book and quoting example code does not require permission. Incorporating a significant amount of example code from this book into your product's documentation does require permission.

We appreciate, but do not require, attribution. An attribution usually includes the title, author, publisher, and ISBN. For example: "*Design Patterns*, by Christopher G. Lasater. Copyright 2007, Wordware Publishing, Inc., 1-59822-031-4."

Acknowledgments

I would like to thank:

The Gang of Four (Erich Gamma, Richard Helm, Ralph Johnson, and John Vlissides) for their research and development of the 23 recognized design patterns.

Martin Fowler for his books and advice.

1

Why Pattern?

Design patterns are basically design tools to improve existing code. Like a carpenter who uses a nail gun instead of a hammer to build a house because he does not hit his thumb and can nail a house together in days instead of weeks, design patterns allow the code you write to be easier to implement, build, and maintain. They are tools to improve efficiency but more importantly allow you as the developer to improve your overall design skills as well as the quality of your projects, and give you a wider scope of skill sets. They allow you to see new answers to common and specialized problems. They define a common programming model, which can translate across to other developers also familiar with patterns. They standardize common programming tasks into recognizable forms, giving your projects better cohesiveness. In general, they help to make you a better designer.

Common Aspects of Object-Oriented Languages

Design pattern models are based and depend highly on the aspects of object-oriented languages. That is to say that patterns-based programming doesn't make much sense outside such languages. Aspects of object-oriented languages like encapsulation, polymorphism, abstraction, and inheritance all extend their properties into patterns-based coding. You might say that patterns methodology is an extension of object-oriented methodology. To better understand where patterns fit into the object-oriented world, we need to examine some of these properties.

Encapsulation is one of the most important aspects of object-oriented languages. The rule of encapsulation is one of keeping things private or masked inside the domain of an object, package, namespace, class, or interface and allowing only expected access to pieces of functionality. We use the rule of encapsulation in almost every aspect of OOP (object-oriented programming). This rule allows us to build patterns like facades, proxies, bridges, and adapters. It allows us to hide with an interface or class structure some functionality that we do not wish to be publicly or globally known. It allows us to define scope inside our programs, and helps us to define and group modules of logic. It provides ways to allow objects to communicate without that communication getting either too complex or too entangled. It provides rules of engagement between different code bases, and helps us decide what functionality can be known and what needs to be hidden.

Think of encapsulation like your mortgage company. You send off your mortgage payment every month and get a statement back showing your loan data. How your payment is applied and handled inside the mortgage company's accounting department is unknown to you, but you can see evidence of it in your statements and the slowly reducing loan debt against your house. The accounting processes behind how this process works is invisible to you. It exists behind the business facade of the mortgage company. The company has processes and rules based on laws and business practices to guarantee that your money is safely deposited and applied to your loan. You know it works; you just don't know or even care *how* it works, as long as it works as expected and returns the expected results.

Working with encapsulation within your programs is very similar to the example we just read. Let's say we want to build a class that applies your mortgage payment to your loan. We obviously want to allow limited access to this class, since it handles money and sensitive information, so allowing every process around it to access every method inside it would not be a good idea. So instead we choose two methods to make public and mark the access of the remaining methods private. One of the public methods is a method to apply the payments, including the money and account number as input parameters and outputting the loan amount left after the payment is applied. The other is a method to return amortized data surrounding the payment plan.

```
class CustomerPayment
{
    public double PostPayment(int loanId, double payment)
    {
        .....performs post of payment to customer account
```

```
    }

    public ArrayList GetAmortizedSchedule(int loanId)
    {
        ...returns an amortization schedule in array
    }
}
```

Notice that the two methods in the code above are visible as public. We can assume that the `CustomerPayment` class has many other methods and code to help perform some of the functions of its two public methods, but since we cannot access them outside the class code they are in effect invisible to any other classes in the code domain. This gives us proper encapsulation of the class methods, allowing only the required methods to be accessed. Thus, the method of encapsulation for this class is to allow only the two methods, `PostPayment()` and `GetAmortizedSchedule()`, to be accessed outside the class.

Polymorphism is another important aspect of object-oriented programming. The rule of polymorphism states that classes can be altered according to their state, in effect making them a different object based on values of attributes, type, or function. We use polymorphism in almost every coding situation, especially patterns. This rule gives us the power to use abstraction and inheritance, allowing inherited members to change according to how they implement their base class. It also allows us to change a class's purpose and function based on its current state. Polymorphism helps interfaces change their implementation class type simply by allowing several different classes to use the same interface. Polymorphic declarations of specific implementations of classes with a common base or interface are extremely common in object-oriented code.

To better understand polymorphism we can think of an example of using an interface and a group of classes that implement the interface to perform different functionality for different implementations.

> **Note**   An *interface* is a type of code that is not a class, but acts together with different classes to define a common link, which would not be possible otherwise. It is simply a protocol in object-oriented languages that exists between classes and objects to provide an agreed upon linkage.

Let's take a look at an example that illustrates the role polymorphism plays in a relationship between classes without a common base class and an interface designed to allow some common definitions between these classes.

We start out with some common if...then...else code as we might see in any language, either scripting or object. Our mission is to use the aspect of polymorphism to make this code more flexible.

```
if(IsAntiqueAuto)
    AntiqueAuto auto = new AntiqueAuto();
    int cylinders = auto.Cylinders();
    int numDoors = auto.NumberDoors();
    int year = auto.Year();
    string make = auto.Make();
    string model = auto.Model();
}
```

The first thing you need to answer is why do we want to change this code? The answer might be one of portability: You wish to have many car types and pass the logic of creating them via the class itself, rather than via a logical Boolean statement. Or you might wish to make sure all auto classes have the same methods so your code accessing the object always knows what to expect.

In the code example below we can see an interface, IAuto, and below it some classes that we have modified to implement this interface. We can assume that each class also implements the interface's methods, each functioning in its own way, returning values according to the logic specific to the implemented methods on each class.

```
public interface IAuto
{
    int Cylinders();
    int NumberDoors();
    int Year();
    string Make();
    string Model();
}
class AntiqueAuto : IAuto....

class SportsCar : IAuto....

class Sedan : IAuto.....

class SUV : IAuto.....
```

To understand how polymorphism acts in the interface-class relationship, let's look at some code where different class types are created via the IAuto interface. First, we see how one of the classes that implement the interface methods can use the interface to define each class's methods as independent logic. Let's look at an example of one of the classes we saw in the previous code example. Notice that each of the methods that are present in the interface are represented in the `AntiqueAuto` implementation and return values specific to its type of auto. This is mandated by the compiler, to ensure all methods in the interface are implemented in the class to determine common functionality between this class and others that implement the `IAuto` interface. This defines one aspect of polymorphism, in that by changing its underlying class type, the interface can allow different functionality from each class implementation.

```
class AntiqueAuto : IAuto
{
    public int Cylinders()
    {
        return 4;
    }
    public int NumberDoors()
    {
        return 3;
    }
    public int Year()
    {
        return 1905;
    }
    public string Make()
    {
        return "Ford";
    }
    public string Model()
    {
        return "Model T";
    }
}
```

Now, when looking at another class that implements the same interface, we see it has a completely different implementation of each of the interface methods:

```
//another implementation of IAuto
class SportsCar : IAuto
{
    public int Cylinders()
    {
        return 8;
    }
    public int NumberDoors()
    {
        return 2;
    }
    public int Year()
    {
        return 2005;
    }
    public string Make()
    {
        return "Porsche";
    }
    public string Model()
    {
        return "Boxter";
    }
}
```

Next, we instantiate the AntiqueAuto class as an instance of the IAuto interface and call each of the interface methods. Each method returns a value from the methods implemented on the AntiqueAuto class.

```
IAuto auto = new AntiqueAuto();
int cylinders = auto.Cylinders();
int numDoors = auto.NumberDoors();
int year = auto.Year();
string make = auto.Make();
string model = auto.Model();
```

If we changed the implemented class to `SportsCar` or another auto type, the methods would return different values. This is how polymorphism comes into play in class relationships. By changing the class type for a common interface or abstraction, we can change the functionality and scope of the code without having to code `if...then...else` statements to accomplish the same thing.

```
IAuto auto = new SportsCar();
int cylinders = auto.Cylinders();
int numDoors = auto.NumberDoors();
int year = auto.Year();
string make = auto.Make();
string model = auto.Model();
```

Inheritance and abstraction are also very important features of object-oriented languages. They provide a way to make polymorphic representations of objects and object relationships that can be managed at run time or compile time.

Inheritance is the ability of one object to be derived by creating a new class instance from a parent or base class and overloading the constructor(s), methods, and attributes of that parent object and implementing them in the instance. In Java this is known as *subclassing*. Inheritance is important because many times an object contains some base functionality that another object also needs and, instead of maintaining the same logic in two objects, they can share and even override or change this functionality by using a base or parent class. If this occurs, then the base or parent object should be defined in such a way that several common derived objects can use the same common functionality from the parent. The parent should only contain functionality common to *all* its children.

Abstraction is the actual method in which we use inheritance. *Abstraction* is the ability to abstract into a base class some common functionality or design that is common to several *implementation* or instanced classes. The difference — in this book and most code descriptions — between implementation and abstract classes is that abstractions of classes cannot be instanced, while implementations can. Abstraction and inheritance are both aspects of polymorphism, and the reverse is true as well.

> **Note**   Actually there is also a pattern that illustrates this basic relationship. See the "Template Pattern" section in Chapter 3.

Another important aspect of object-oriented languages is how they deal with collections of objects. The equals implementation for objects is an important aspect of dealing with objects inside a collection. Languages like C#, VB.NET, and Java all use this method to help index and compare objects in collections. Let's talk about this briefly.

When a hash table or other collection object indexes and compares an object, it uses the `GetHashCode()` method to help in this indexing and comparison. This method can be overridden to capture a more accurate sampling of the intrinsic properties or state of the object. In other words, the `GetHashCode()` method can return an integer representation of the concatenated state of the properties within an object. If not overridden, then this relationship is less exact. This is important when making comparisons between objects in collection classes like iterators or generic collection objects like hash tables. You need to make accurate representations of the internal state of objects so the correct object can be compared or indexed in a collection.

There are general rules to guarantee that each object gets a unique hashing algorithm:

- Objects that compare as equal must return the same hashed value.

- GetHashCode() must return the same value every time, unless the internal value or state is modified.

- The hashed value is not like a GUID (global unique identifier) in that it is not globally unique, but only unique if the hashed algorithm and the object's value are not the same as any other object in the scope of the executing code.

- The default implementation of GetHashCode() in objects that contain state variables or values is not guaranteed to be unique. That is why if uniqueness is desired, then a proper algorithm needs to be implemented in the overridden method on a particular class.

- To provide a complete representation of state, the values of each variable that represents the object's state need to be part of the hashing algorithm.

To illustrate the proper way to implement the GetHashCode() method, take a look at this example:

```
public override int GetHashCode()
{
    return _name.GetHashCode() ^ _address.GetHashCode();
}
```

We see that the method has been overridden, and two instance variables have been concatenated with the ^ symbol and returned as their sum. Another way to do this is with the + sign, which returns the same result:

```
public override int GetHashCode()
{
    return _name.GetHashCode() + _address.GetHashCode();
}
```

Taking all the variables that may change the state of the object and returning their concatenated hashed values guarantees that each object will have unique values based on state. This allows objects used as keys in collections like hash tables to act in the proper manner.

The `Equals(object obj)` method is the required method for *bitwise* comparisons of value objects. It is especially useful in sorting collections or when a comparison operation is desired in a collection. Not all primitive or object types can have bitwise equality, and so those are compared by value, as in the case of decimal 2.2000 and 2.2, which have the same value but different binary equality.

The proper operational sequence usually starts with a null check, then a class type comparison, and then a comparison of all the value types (or reference types) that influence the state of the class:

```
public override bool Equals(object obj)
{
    if(obj != null && obj is Component)
        return _name.Equals(((Component)obj).Name) &&
        _address.Equals(((Component)obj).Address);
    else
        return false;
}
```

There are some basic rules when testing the equals implementation for proper return values:

■ `obj1.Equals(obj1) = true` — an object always equals itself.

■ `obj1.Equals(obj2) = obj2.Equals(obj1)` — equals implementations across different class instances always return true on both classes if equal.

■ `obj1.Equals(obj2) && obj2.Equals(obj3) && obj3.Equals(obj1) = true` — if object 1 is equal to object 2 and object 2 is equal to object 3, then object 3 must be equal to object 1.

■ All calls to `Equals()` return the same value unless the class's state or internal value is modified.

■ `Equals(null)` always returns false.

Patterns Cross-Reference Each Other

One interesting thing about design patterns is that they can complement or redefine each other. As you read the examples and sections in this book, you will notice that I include a paragraph in each section that refers to other patterns and provides some comparisons between these patterns. This is because, like aspects of object-oriented programming that work in a cohesive manner, design patterns often use and reference each other to accomplish common goals. You may also find when using design patterns other new patterns spring to life by morphing two of the known patterns. Don't get too excited though! It is a sure bet most of the morphed patterns have already been invented in some form, so yours might not be the first implementation. This is true of code in general. It has been said that there are no new inventions, just new combinations, and the same could be said of code.

Refactoring Legacy Code and Improving New Code

As you read through this book, you will see many instances in the problems sections of each chapter that start out with code mannerisms that may be familiar to you. Boolean logical code seems to be where people who are just learning patterns seem to have a common reference. Almost everyone who writes code starts out with `if...then...else` code.

If you have ever spent hours trying to write a complex set of algorithms and ended up with spaghetti code, you have probably realized the shortcomings of writing solely in Boolean logic. I wrote this book keeping in mind that people who might have an interest in patterns probably would not have a primer to interpret and decide where a pattern might fit into their code. So in each example of the 23 patterns I start out with simple Boolean logic code (or `if...then...else`) if I can, and I then demonstrate a *refactoring* effort toward that particular pattern. I do this both to demonstrate how the pattern fits into real-world code and to give you a lesson on how to perform upgrades to your code through refactoring.

Reflection and OOP

For those not familiar with how reflection works on classes, think of the IntelliSense drop-downs in your IDE and how they display classes, methods, parameters, and attributes. IntelliSense uses reflection on the class types to provide this information. Basically, *reflection* is a way to look at your class types through a run-time API and determine their location, structure, and type. Using reflection in code can be a useful tool. If you want a looser coupling of code bases, reflection can be a key component to providing this functionality. Creating classes without defining their type until run time is useful in many ways. If you did not have reflection methods in your language API, doing this would be hard, if not impossible. Reflection can be used in place of compiled code relationships to make your code more dynamic. There are a few examples in this book that use reflection. I make use of reflection to extend some of the pattern examples where this is appropriate. I do this to provide some coding solutions that are not usually part of patterns texts, but are good examples of implementations of real-world solutions.

2

Creational Patterns

Creational patterns are patterns whose sole purpose is to facilitate the work of creating, initializing, and configuring objects and classes. They are grouped thus by the Gang of Four (Erich Gamma, Richard Helm, Ralph Johnson, and John Vlissides), who are the individuals originally responsible for formalizing the accepted design patterns we use today. Basically, creational patterns are grouped thus because they create things: other classes, interface implementations, attributes, or any other structural type. They basically act as factories, builders, configuration constructs, or class initializers. These types of patterns are useful when we need to render instances of objects, store these objects, perform complex initialization of objects, or create copies of objects.

Factory Pattern

What Is a Factory Pattern?

Factories are just what their name implies: they are classes that create or construct something. In the case of object-oriented code languages, this means they construct and return an instance of a class type. They provide an encapsulation of code required to render an instance of an abstract class type as an implementation class. The factory can initialize, pull in data, configure, set state, and perform nearly any other creational operation needed for a class.

As stated above, factories use a base class type to create a class instance. This type can be in the form of either an abstraction or an interface, and based on that type, via creational methods, the factory renders a functional class that inherits or implements this type.

Let's talk about some ways to use a factory that you might find useful. You might use a Factory pattern if you had a lot of creational logic for instances of a class type strewn throughout your code base. You might wish to consolidate this logic into one place for uniformity and maintainability. Instead of having to change logic in many places when you want to modify how the class is created, you could move it into a factory. Then you could change it in one place inside the factory instead of hunting through your code.

A factory might also be useful when you want to limit and define the accepted member implementations of a certain abstract class type for a particular logical flow, but do not want to define at compile time the logic for which type might be used. For example, you might pass in a key to the factory method instead of using a Boolean `if...then... else` statement to determine the class you want to construct and return from your factory. Doing that would free you from having to use compiled Boolean statements and instead allow something outside your factory to determine the logical flow of which implementation of a class type is rendered.

Factories can be static or creation only, or *repositories*, which both create and store references to the created products. But in general, factories provide a way to house the creational aspects of class types.

The *Factory* pattern has two main components: the *Factory* and the *Product*. The factory class is the class that renders the product class. The product class is the class containing data or functionality and is part of a series of class types that can be rendered from a factory method as an instance of an abstract type.

Let's take a look at some problems that you might encounter when working with your legacy code or creating new code, and how the Factory pattern can help.

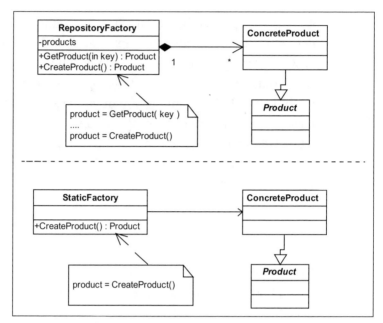

Figure 2-1. UML for Factory pattern

Problem 1: Implementation classes with a common base are created in multiple places and no uniformity exists between creational logic

To illustrate the usefulness of the Factory pattern in functional code, let's define a common problem that you might find within your code. Let's say we have several classes that need to be created that have a common base or abstract class. These classes are currently constructed throughout your legacy code in different places, which creates a maintenance problem:

```
.....lives in class FindSuit
Suit suit;
if(suitType == SuitType.Armani)
    suit = new Armani();
else if(suitType == SuitType.StripedBusinessSuit)
    suit = new StripedBusinessSuit();

.....lives in class GetSuit
if(suitType == SuitType.PlaidBusinessSuit)
    suit = new PlaidBusinessSuit();
else if(suitType == SuitType.GolfSuit)
    suit = new GolfSuit();
```

As you can see by the example above, we build a different implementation of Suit based on the value of a defined type as an *enum*, SuitType. We use Suit as a *contract* for the returned implementation type. The Suit class is an abstract class that defines all implementations for a suit, including common attributes and methods. The problem is that we do not have any central place to house all this creational logic and the code can be messy and lacks uniformity, which causes poor maintainability. (You can see in the example that the if...then...else code block exists in multiple places throughout the code.)

Creational Patterns *(side tab)*

Solution 1: Use a factory to encapsulate the class creation code in one place

The first step in improving our existing code base and solving our maintenance and functional issues regarding our legacy code is to encapsulate the creation and decisional process of which type of the Suit class to create, giving us a central repository to house the conditional code. We use the Factory pattern to perform this encapsulation.

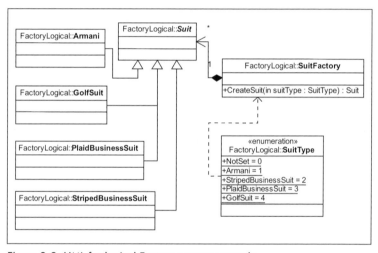

Figure 2-2. UML for logical Factory pattern example

The factory will allow us a singular place for the creational logic, solving the issue of maintaining the code in several places. It will also allow us to refine and expand the code in this one place, guaranteeing that calls from different access points within the code will render similar results. This decreases the number of bugs the code may contain *and* decreases the scope of making changes to the creational logic. In other words, if we need to change or add to the ways we can create a Suit, we need only do it inside the factory, instead of searching all over our code to make these changes, possibly missing some places or making these changes without uniformity.

> **Note**   Notice in the code example below that we have identified our factory with the class accessor `sealed`. This is done to keep other classes from inheriting from the factory, which prevents any abstractions. It also ensures that we are dealing with a single known instance of `SuitFactory` that works the same across any implementation.

Here we see the Boolean logical code we have refactored inside our factory class:

```
public sealed class SuitFactory
{
    public Suit CreateSuit(SuitType suitType)
    {
        Suit suit;
        if(suitType == SuitType.Armani)
            suit = new Armani();
        else if(suitType == SuitType.StripedBusinessSuit)
            suit = new StripedBusinessSuit();
        else if(suitType == SuitType.PlaidBusinessSuit)
            suit = new PlaidBusinessSuit();
        else if(suitType == SuitType.GolfSuit)
            suit = new GolfSuit();
        return suit;
    }
}
```

Now we need to clean up all our different areas where the creational logic for `Suit` exists, and replace these references with the call to the factory:

```
.....refactored in class FindSuit & GetSuit
SuitFactory factory = new SuitFactory();
Suit suit = factory.CreateSuit(SuitType.Armani);
```

We have now successfully cleaned up the code base and improved maintainability and scalability of the creational logic for all `Suit` implementations. We can test the new code and see that we return only the expected type:

```
Suit:Armani
```

But we now have another problem. The factory has a scalability issue regarding the conditional logic stored within. To add new implementation classes that subclass `Suit`, we still have to change the conditional logic inside the factory. Also, we cannot define for the scope of the factory, only the required implementations of `Suit` that we wish to deal with. In the next section we will discuss how to make some improvements to resolve these issues, and how we might use reflection to improve our code.

Problem 2: Class types to be created are determined by immutable logical code and extending the returnable types requires scale modifications to the factory

Now that we have our factory class built and all our legacy code migrated to use the factory, the next problem is that we want to expand the logical if...then...else code. This presents a scalability issue, due to the fact that we are limited within the design to only the types included within the conditional logic, and cannot readily expand the accepted types without modifying this logic. Examine the example below. Notice we have added some new types to return from the factory. This code block could become unwieldy, especially if we want to expand into initialization or configuration of the class types before rendering them from the factory.

```
public sealed class SuitFactory
{
    public Suit CreateSuit(SuitType suitType)
    {
        Suit suit;
        if(suitType == SuitType.Armani)
            suit = new Armani();
        else if(suitType == SuitType.StripedBusinessSuit)
            suit = new StripedBusinessSuit();
        else if(suitType == SuitType.PlaidBusinessSuit)
            suit = new PlaidBusinessSuit();
        else if(suitType == SuitType.GolfSuit)
            suit = new GolfSuit();
        else if(suitType == SuitType.MotorcycleSuit)//added type
            suit = new MotorcycleSuit();
        else if(suitType == SuitType.JoggingSuit)//added type
            suit = new JoggingSuit();
```

```
        else if(suitType == SuitType.LadiesPantsSuit)//added type
            suit = new LadiesPantsSuit();
        else if(suitType == SuitType.SolidBusinessSuit)//added type
            suit = new SolidBusinessSuit();
        else if(suitType == SuitType.TennisSuit)//added type
            suit = new TennisSuit();

        return suit;
    }
}
```

We also need to somehow maintain the class types within the factory. We do not wish to load them each time they are called.

There are two solutions for this problem, and each is covered in its own solution section that follows. Read both sections before making your factory decision. The first uses reflected types to determine the accepted classes for the workflow. The second uses inheritance to accomplish the same goal. The first solution is something that is widely used in factories of all types in many different coding languages. Our second solution is closer to the original adaptation of the pattern by the Gang of Four.

Solution 2a: Replace conditional logic with a class activator, using reflection to determine the needed types for different workflows

Encapsulating the logic into a single location inside the SuitFactory class solves the issue of maintaining multiple code bases for the same logic, but we still have a lot of conditional Boolean logic code inside the factory that deals with the creational process. This means that our factory has a scalability issue, in that we have to now house logic for every possible solution rather than just those for the scope of the current workflow. This presents the same maintenance issue as before: with expansion or addition to the code we have to make compile changes to the factory conditional logic. This we will need to change as well since it is very hard to maintain and, with every new class type, we need to add a new code block to the `if...then... else` code. Also, the factory should be relatively dumb in regard to the actual implementation of the `Suit` class. That is, the factory should not have to make direct differentiations between different types; the abstract class itself should be the interface for doing that by using the polymorphic properties of the abstraction of the `Suit` class into its implementation classes. This is important because it allows the object-oriented language's polymorphism property to interact with the logical flow, freeing immutable logical flow back into objects. Polymorphism of the classes removes the need to specify the class type, which allows new class types to be added to the factory in an ad-hoc fashion, provided they inherit from the `Suit` base class. This moves the scope back into implementing only the needed classes for each workflow. To accomplish this we can use an instance creation mechanism based on a reflected type and a type registry.

> **Note**   Notice in the UML below that the actual implementation classes do not change from our previous solution. We simply change how the factory builds them. The factory methods do not need to change either. We will simply replace the Boolean logical code with the reflective algorithm.

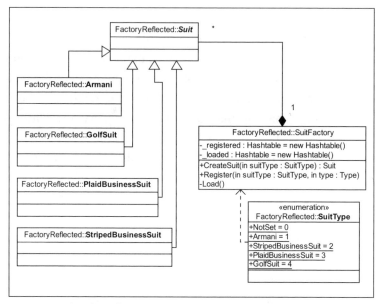

Figure 2-3. UML for reflection Factory pattern example

We add into our factory two dictionary lists: one to house registered types keyed with the `SuitType` enum, and one for housing the loaded `Suit` implementation classes. We use a lazy load method to load the registered class types upon first call to the `CreateSuit()` method. *Lazy loading* is a technique by which data is only loaded when a method to access data is called, instead of doing it at process start.

```
private Hashtable _registered = new Hashtable();
private Hashtable _loaded = new Hashtable();

public Suit CreateSuit(SuitType suitType)
{
    //if the value is null we either have registered
    //a new type and not loaded it, or this is the first load
    if(_loaded[suitType] == null)
        Load();//lazy loaded on first call to method
    return (Suit)_loaded[];
}
```

To identify the proper class implementations of Suit for the workflow in which the factory is being called and only those implementations, we add a registry method to identify which implementation types of Suit are allowed. The registry method in the example ties together the enum with the class type, conforming to the legacy code's already present data standards, but allowing typed reflection to be used in place of the Boolean logic to determine the class implementation of Suit to be returned from the factory. This is accomplished by entering the enum as a key and the reflected type data as a value into a dictionary object, which holds the key-value pairs.

```
public void Register(SuitType suitType, Type type)
{
    _registered.Add(suitType, type);
}
```

We will use reflection to interact with the keyed types we store in the registry to actually build our Suit classes. Reflection sometimes has been argued as being inefficient, but when used properly, it can be an invaluable tool in object-oriented languages that support it. Let's talk about some types of reflective tools in languages, and how they

Creational Patterns

can be used in the factory to both identify the class types and create them.

The `Activator` class in .NET is useful for creating instances of classes by using their type and any input parameters needed for the constructor. In our case we don't have any constructor parameters, so we just pass in the type:

```
Type type = typeof(GolfSuit);
Suit suit = (Suit)Activator.CreateInstance(type));
```

Java uses reflection to do the same thing using the `java.lang.reflect.Constructor` package. Using a reflection method that takes the parameter types and builds the class implementation based on a constructor that matches both the class type and input parameter types, a class is built from a reflection constructor mechanism:

```
Constructor con = Class.forName("GolfSuit").getConstructor(null);
return con.newInstance(null);
```

.NET also has such a reflection constructor, `Type.Get-Constructor`, which takes the parameter types and builds the class implementation based on a constructor that matches both the class type and input parameter types passed into the `GetConstructor()` method. It then uses the `ConstructorInfo.Invoke()` method, passing the parameter values to actually create the class instance:

```
Type type = typeof(GolfSuit);
ConstructorInfo info = type.GetConstructor(new Type[]{});
Suit suit = (Suit)info.Invoke(new object[]{}));
```

Any of these methods are acceptable. The main aspect to understand is that the actual expected type from reflection is needed to create a class, instead of hard compiling the class type declaration in the logical Boolean code.

Let's take a look at the entire factory, with the registry and load methods. Notice how the `CreateSuit()` method has changed. Now no conditional logic is present, and there are no direct class declarations. We have extracted this using direct reflection upon the registered types, and allowed the workflow to determine which of those types it needs to deal with. We are lazy loading the classes all at once when either the first call to the method is made or we register a new class not yet loaded.

```
public sealed class SuitFactory
{
    private Hashtable _registered = new Hashtable();
    private Hashtable _loaded = new Hashtable();
```

Our actual factory create method receives as an input parameter the `SuitType` enum and returns the class instance from the loaded collection. If no value exists, we load the entire collection.

```
public Suit CreateSuit(SuitType suitType)
{
    if(_loaded[suitType] == null)
        Load();
    return (Suit)_loaded[suitType];
}
```

Our registry method gives us a way to determine the allowed types for the particular process we are running. We call this method on initialization of our factory and before the first call to the `CreateSuit()` method.

```
public void Register(SuitType suitType, Type type)
{
    _registered.Add(suitType, type);
}
```

Our `Load()` method constructs all the types registered with the `Register()` method we saw above and loads them into the collection. The factory performs the actual loading of the registered types using reflection on the class type from the values in the registry dictionary object. The loaded type is defined by stating an expected base type of `Suit`, and the implementation class is loaded by its type with the `SuitType` enum as the dictionary key.

```
private void Load()
{
    foreach(DictionaryEntry obj in _registered)
    {
        Type type = (Type)obj.Value;
        ConstructorInfo info = type.GetConstructor(new Type[]{});
        if(!_loaded.ContainsKey(obj.Key))
        //checks if the class is loaded
            _loaded.Add(obj.Key,(Suit)info.Invoke(new
                           object[]{}));
            //we can use direct reflection in .NET or an activator
        //_loaded.Add(obj.Key,(Suit)Activator.CreateInstance(type));
    }

}
```

Another way to do this without sharing the instances is to create new classes with every call to the `CreateSuit()` method. We might do this if we did not desire any state for our instance variables. Be careful when dealing with dictionaries, especially hash tables, as they keep a reference to your class objects and store changes to those classes within themselves. If you want a class to have freshly initialized data every time you call an instance from the factory, create a new class with every call to the factory. If, on the other hand, you would like to maintain the state of your classes between calls to the factory, such a dictionary object might serve your purposes.

Finally, let's look at where and how in your legacy code the factory can be implemented, replacing the existing conditional logic code used in different places. First, we must declare the particular instance of the factory we need. Next, we register only the needed class types we wish to return from the factory. After that, we can create our implementation of `Suit`, passing in the `SuitType` enum that our conditional logic used before.

```
SuitFactory factory = new SuitFactory();
factory.Register(SuitType.Armani, typeof(Armani));
factory.Register(SuitType.GolfSuit, typeof(GolfSuit));
factory.Register(SuitType.PlaidBusinessSuit, typeof
            (PlaidBusinessSuit));
factory.Register(SuitType.StripedBusinessSuit, typeof
            (StripedBusinessSuit));
```

We only define the classes for the current workflow of the factory. This prevents unwanted functionality from appearing during the current workflow. The way we define the classes allowed inside the factory gives us flexibility to change our workflow for each implementation of the factory without changing the internal factory code. Now when we call the factory's creational method, we will only be returning expected results for the context of the factory instance:

```
Suit suit = factory.CreateSuit(SuitType.StripedBusinessSuit);
```

Our test shows us the results of our refactored code:

```
type:Examples.FactoryReflected.StripedBusinessSuit
```

Thus we have illustrated how we can use reflection to help us build our class implementations of `Suit`. We create our classes using reflection upon registered reflection info for a class, instead of immutable logical Boolean code. We also have stored each class instance in the factory, using the factory as a repository for the loaded class types. This meets our requirement for not having to reload a class each time it is called.

We might decide at this point that registering all the classes in one place and providing access to the factory from any thread might better suit our needs. We might make this decision because we see the impact of creating and storing classes across threads using the factory is moot, since we can get separate instances of the class for each thread, and we do not care to have a separate instance of factory for each thread. This might be the case because we would like to preserve the loading state on the factory objects, the use of reflection in the factory needs to be kept to a minimum for greater efficiency, or the classes we load should have their state maintained across multiple threads. In this case, changing the access modifier for the factory by adding the `static` access modifier would allow any thread to access the factory, and keep loading and using reflection inside the factory to a minimum. See the "State Pattern" section in Chapter 3 for details on this.

This solution is one way of using a factory, and generally the most common way when a simple class type needs to be implemented. In the next solution we will look at another way in which the Factory pattern is utilized, using inheritance instead of reflection to identify the accepted class types for a workflow.

Solution 2b: Use abstractions of the factory to determine allowable class types using inheritance (instead of reflection)

Another way we could determine which classes are available from each factory instance without using an outside registry method or reflection is to use abstractions of the factory, and inside those abstractions determine the allowable class type implementations for each factory type.

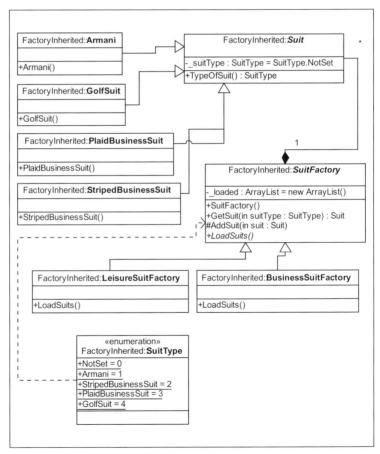

Figure 2-4. UML for inherited Factory pattern example

To do this we would need to make `SuitFactory` abstract, and inherit from it the factories for the individual workflows that will define the class implementations of `Suit` that can be allowed in each inherited implementation. That is, we will inherit from a base factory class, and each inherited member will be defined by loading the allowed class types of `Suit`. All factory methods to return the `Suit` implementation classes will be included in the abstract `SuitFactory` class with one exception: `LoadSuits()`.

`LoadSuits()` is an abstract method that is to be implemented in the inherited members of `SuitFactory`, and is where we determine which classes will be allowed to be returned from the factory. Instead of using reflection to determine the class types, or a Boolean code block as in the previous examples, we use inheritance and polymorphism. We call the `LoadSuits()` method inside the abstract `SuitFactory`'s constructor to maintain a maximum of functionality in the abstract, and prevent duplicate code from making its way into the inherited members.

Below we see the class has a private collection of type `ArrayList`. This is to be used to hold the loaded class instances. It is marked private to control access in its inherited members. A little later we will create a protected method to allow loading of class instances to the collection.

```
public abstract class SuitFactory
{
    private ArrayList _loaded = new ArrayList();
```

In our constructor we call the `LoadSuits()` method. This ensures our classes that override the `LoadSuits()` method will have the desired implementations loaded.

```
public SuitFactory()
{
    LoadSuits();
}
```

Here the `GetSuit()` method returns a concrete `Suit` class instance. The returned class instance has a property `TypeOfSuit` that matches the passed-in parameter of `SuitType`:

```
public Suit GetSuit(SuitType suitType)
{
    Suit suit = null;
    foreach(Suit obj in _loaded)
    {
        if(obj.TypeOfSuit == suitType)
        {
            suit = obj;
            break;
        }
    }
    return suit;
}
```

Here we include a way to add the suits directly to the collection. The method is marked protected so that only inherited members can access the method:

```
protected void AddSuit(Suit suit)
{
    _loaded.Add(suit);
}
```

Finally, we create our abstract method `LoadSuits()`. This method will be overridden in the inherited factory classes to tell us what type of classes we will be allowed to return from our factory.

```
public abstract void LoadSuits();
}
```

Here we see one class that will inherit our abstract
`SuitFactory` class. Because of the way we built that
abstract base, we only need to override the `LoadSuits()`
method and load the allowed classes into the underlying
collection using our protected `AddSuit()` method.

```
//inherited factory from SuitFactory
public class LeisureSuitFactory : SuitFactory
{
    public override void LoadSuits()
    {
        this.AddSuit(new GolfSuit());
    }
}
```

We can now create a variety of inherited classes from our
abstract `SuitFactory` class. Each one will contain the
same override of the `LoadSuits()` method, where we can
determine the correct types of classes we wish to return. In
the class below, we see we are loading three new class
instances. Each concrete factory class can define its own
implementation by simply loading the class in the overridden method.

```
//inherited factory from SuitFactory
public class BusinessSuitFactory : SuitFactory
{
    public override void LoadSuits()
    {
        this.AddSuit(new PlaidBusinessSuit());
        this.AddSuit(new StripedBusinessSuit());
        this.AddSuit(new Armani());
    }
}
```

So we still have only the desired implementations for `Suit`
for each workflow, and we use the appropriate inherited

member of `SuitFactory` to determine which types are available for each workflow or code process flow:

```
LeisureSuitFactory lfactory = new LeisureSuitFactory();
BusinessSuitFactory bfactory = new BusinessSuitFactory();
```

Since we are allowing the concrete implementations of `SuitFactory` to determine which types are available for each workflow or code process flow, we are confident only the allowed instances of `Suit` will be returned from each factory instance:

```
Suit lsuit = lfactory.GetSuit(SuitType.GolfSuit);
Suit bsuit = bfactory.GetSuit(SuitType.PlaidBusinessSuit);
```

We can see by our test we indeed return the expected concrete implementations of `Suit` for each type:

```
Factory:Examples.FactoryInherited.LeisureSuitFactory
        Suit type:Examples.FactoryInherited.GolfSuit
Factory:Examples.FactoryInherited.BusinessSuitFactory
        Suit type:Examples.FactoryInherited.PlaidBusinessSuit
```

Comparison to Similar Patterns

Factories work well when returning a class type that is based on a base class. If, however, you need to perform several operations to create an object, a Builder pattern might be more appropriate. If you need uniformity over several factories to do the same work, consider an Abstract Factory pattern.

What We Have Learned

We saw in the solutions above that we could easily encapsulate the logical creation of classes of a determined type inside a factory class, giving us better uniformity and maintainability of the creational code. We also learned that we could change the scale and scope of the classes a factory could handle, depending on its implementation, using reflection and a registry method or by inheriting different factory implementations to define the required return types for each workflow. When working with inherited factory instances to control the workflow, we determined that each instance of the factory could react differently, depending on how it was set up for that code flow instance, and could render inherited classes from a common base class type.

Related Patterns

- Abstract Factory pattern
- Builder pattern
- Flyweight pattern
- Interpreter pattern
- Prototype pattern
- State pattern
- Template pattern

Abstract Factory Pattern

What Is an Abstract Factory Pattern?

The *Abstract Factory* pattern is a creative way to expand on the basic Factory pattern. Since the Factory pattern is a class that creates other classes in a uniform way, the Abstract Factory pattern gives us a way to allow factories with similar methods and access points to be interchangeable. That is, using an abstract factory we can define implementation class types as factories with the abstract factory as the base, and thereby tie in all the different factory implementations to a base class.

So now that we have a basic explanation of what an abstract factory is, let's talk about how this is useful in our code. Let's start by discussing what factories actually do in code and why they are valuable.

A factory class is a way to compartmentalize code that creates other classes and types. It can initialize, pull in data, configure, set state, and perform nearly any other creational operation needed. An abstract factory then is generally used when you may have multiple factories that do different things for a class type, and you wish to provide uniformity between these factories. So let's say you have two different factories. Each one has slightly different creational logic and renders a particular class type. If each of these factories rendered the same class type, but differed in how they create the class type as an instance, we could tie both those factories together using an abstract factory class as a base. Now if we wanted to use the two factory classes interchangeably for different situations but still return the same class type, we could do so without having to rewrite the code that calls the factory to explicitly call a particular factory class type.

The Abstract Factory pattern has two main components: the *Abstract Factory* and the *Abstract Product*. The abstract factory class holds the definition for creating the concrete implementations of the factory, including the abstract method references. The abstract product class is the definition for the concrete implementations of the class that the factory renders.

Let's take a look at some problems that you might encounter when working with your legacy code or creating new code, and how the Abstract Factory pattern can help.

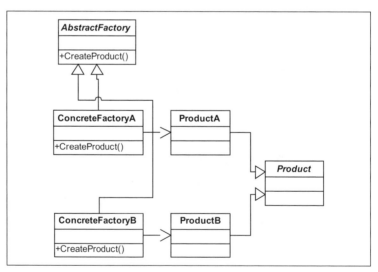

Figure 2-5. UML for Abstract Factory pattern

Problem 1: Different class types need a common interface to a factory method for creation of internal attributes

For our real-world code problem for this pattern we have a class that, depending on its type, needs a different factory to fill its attributes. Let's say we also might want to be able to uniformly define which creation methods we can call on each factory in order to provide a common structure between factory implementations. So let's look at the current problem in code:

```
if(obj is ImageClass)
    obj.Attributes = ImageFactory().GetImageAttributes();

else if(obj.GetType() == typeof(TextClass))
    obj.Attributes = TextFactory().GetTextAttributes();
```

Notice that we have an `if...then...else` statement that determines by the object's class type which factory to use to fill in its attributes. We can assume for this example that the different object type classes of the `Attributes` accessor have a uniform or common base class, which gives us the accessible parameter `Attributes`. In this case the base type of `Attributes` is a hash table.

Our problem then is that we have no cohesion between factories and are forced to use different methods depending on the type of factory. We also have to change code in multiple places (assuming the `if...then...else` code block above exists in multiple places throughout your code), which presents a maintenance issue. We also might want to add some more types of objects and factories and do not want to have a long and cumbersome logical statement with repeating code.

Creational Patterns

Solution 1: Allow an abstract factory to act as a common base interface for the factories between classes

To provide uniformity between polymorphic class types we usually use some sort of contract, in this case we use an abstraction contract: the abstract factory. The abstract factory defines the common creation methods between the factories, allowing a polymorphic generation of objects depending on the factory implementation.

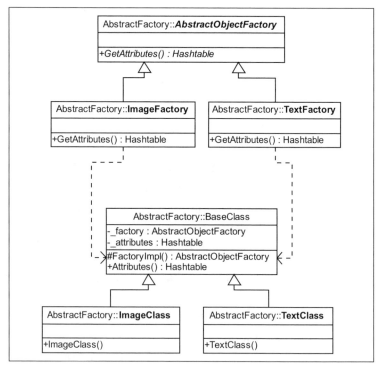

Figure 2-6. UML for Abstract Factory example

The particular problem in the previous section illustrates a lack of polymorphic cohesion between factories. We stated a need for a common interface between factories due to the need for additions to the existing code and a common way to introduce attribute values. To accomplish this we first need to establish the base factory as the contract:

```
abstract class AbstractObjectFactory
{
    abstract public Hashtable GetAttributes();
}
```

Notice the common abstract method on the `AbstractObjectFactory` for returning the attributes, `GetAttributes()`. This method defines how all implementations of the abstract factory will be formed, and how any access to the implementation factory will be handled. This gives us common uniformity between polymorphic instances of each factory.

Next, we need to make this abstract factory the base for the implementation factories, in effect inheriting each from `AbstractObjectFactory` and setting up the specialized factory code inside the overridden `GetAttributes()` method:

```
class ImageFactory : AbstractObjectFactory
{
    public override Hashtable GetAttributes()
        //changed from GetImageAttributes
    {
        Hashtable attributes = new Hashtable();
        attributes["height"] = 52;
        attributes["width"] = 100;
        attributes["imageUrl"] = "http://imageserver/images/
                              someimage.gif";
```

```
        return attributes;

    }
}
```

Each concrete implementation of the Abstract-
ObjectFactory class can have its own logic for how it
returns its expected class type(s). In this case we differ the
contents of our hash table based on which concrete implementation of our abstract factory we are using:

```
class TextFactory : AbstractObjectFactory
{
    public override Hashtable GetAttributes()
        //changed from GetTextAttributes
    {
        Hashtable attributes = new Hashtable();
        attributes["initialText"] = "N/A";
        attributes["maxTextLength"] = 100;
        attributes["textFormat"] = "____@____.__";
        return attributes;

    }
}
```

We need to modify the base class from which ImageClass
and TextClass are inherited. The base class previously
only defined the Attributes parameter, which was the
common object parameter accessor for the two classes.
Now we want to add a private instance for the desired concrete implementation of the AbstractObjectFactory
class:

```
class BaseClass
{

    AbstractObjectFactory _factory;
    Hashtable _attributes;
```

Modifying the base by adding an accessor named
FactoryImpl allows us to pass in any type of factory with
a base of AbstractObjectFactory. This will allow the
particular BaseClass implementation to store its implementation of the AbstractObjectFactory.

```
protected AbstractObjectFactory FactoryImpl
{
    get{return _factory;}
    set{_factory = value;}
}
```

We also change the Attributes parameter, adding a call
to the factory implementation if the attributes are not initialized. This gives us polymorphic cohesion between the
classes for the implementations of AbstractObject-
Factory. This also allows the BaseClass
implementation to house the work of accessing the factory
instead of doing it in external if...then...else
statements.

```
public Hashtable Attributes
{
    get
    {
        if(_attributes == null) _attributes =
            FactoryImpl.GetAttributes();
        return _attributes;
    }
}
```

In the constructor of the implementation classes we define
the type of AbstractObjectFactory we need for each
class type:

```
class ImageClass : BaseClass
{
```

```
public ImageClass()
{
    FactoryImpl = new ImageFactory();
}
}
```

Each concrete implementation of `BaseClass` will define in its constructor the correct factory implementation that is desired for that class:

```
class TextClass : BaseClass
{
    public TextClass()
    {
        FactoryImpl = new TextFactory();
    }
}
```

When we make a call to the implementation of `BaseClass`'s property accessor `Attributes`, we now get the attributes without any need for the conditional logic we started with:

```
ImageClass Attributes:
imageUrl=http://imageserver/images/someimage.gif
width=100
height=52
-------------
TextClass Attributes:
initialText=N/A
maxTextLength=100
textFormat=____  @____.__
```

The original code is no longer necessary, and can be removed from wherever it is located. All factory calls are handled by their particular class type in a lazy load fashion at run time.

Problem 2: We need to make a builder more extendible to allow different functional processes to occur without changing the builder

Another common use for the Abstract Factory pattern is when using a builder. A Builder pattern is another type of creational pattern that provides a way to organize a number of creational methods that initialize or configure a class type before rendering the implementation of that class.

Let's say for this example we have a builder that uses a type of factory: `DuplexFactory`. The builder class uses the factory to create a class representation of a duplex house and initialize all the attributes of that kind of house. Using this particular type of builder, however, we can only build a duplex, since the only factory allowed is the `Duplex-Factory`. But we have a contractor that now builds many other types of houses. For obvious reasons such as scalability of the build process and uniformity of the code that builds a house, we don't want to change the builder class or create a new builder. So we need a way to use the current builder to build any type of house that is needed.

```
public class HouseBuilder
{
    public House Build()
    {
        DuplexFactory factory = new DuplexFactory();
        House house = factory.CreateHouse();
        house.Floor = factory.CreateFloor();
        house.WestWall = factory.CreateWall();
        house.EastWall = factory.CreateWall();
        house.SouthWall = factory.CreateWall();
        house.NorthWall = factory.CreateWall();
        house.Roof = factory.CreateRoof();
        return house;
```

Creational Patterns (sidebar)

```
        }

}
```

Solution 2: Use an abstract factory to define common creational methods for the builder

The first step in analyzing the problem above is to realize that we already have the code inside the builder ready for any implementation of factory that we wish. We only need to abstract the `DuplexFactory`, and make its creational methods abstract methods. This will allow us to create other factories based on these abstract methods.

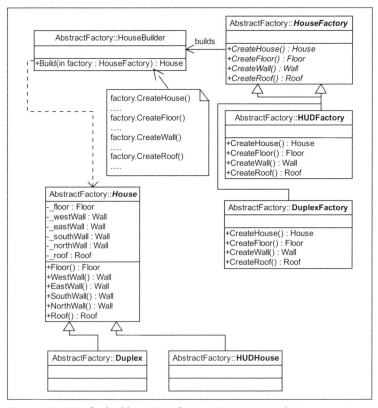

Figure 2-7. UML for builder using Abstract Factory example

Here we see the factory code refactored into the abstract factory class `HouseFactory`:

```
public abstract class HouseFactory
{
    public abstract House CreateHouse();
    public abstract Floor CreateFloor();
    public abstract Wall CreateWall();
    public abstract Roof CreateRoof();


}
```

Notice that each of the methods we saw inside the builder in the problem section's code example is represented here. These abstracted methods give us a *contract*, or common interface, for each implementation of `HouseFactory`, on which we can base inherited factory classes, giving each implementation its own functionality.

Next, we make the different factory classes inherit from `HouseFactory` and implement each of the abstract methods. Each overridden method holds its own representation of the factory code to build its particular type of house.

```
//original factory for duplex
public class DuplexFactory : HouseFactory
{
```

The `CreateHouse()` method creates a new class of type `Duplex`:

```
    public override House CreateHouse()
    {
        return new Duplex();
    }
```

The CreateFloor() method creates a new class of type CementFloor:

```
public override Floor CreateFloor()
{
    return new CementFloor();
}
```

The CreateWall() method creates a new class of type CementBlockWall:

```
public override Wall CreateWall()
{
    return new CementBlockWall();
}
```

The CreateRoof() method creates a new class of type ShingledRoof:

```
public override Roof CreateRoof()
{
    return new ShingledRoof();
}
}
```

Using the abstract factory class HouseFactory we can now implement other factory types. The class below illustrates how by overriding the required abstract methods we can get a completely different set of classes from our factory, all based on their common type:

```
//new factory for different house type
public class HUDFactory : HouseFactory
{
```

The `CreateHouse()` method creates a new class of type `HUDHouse`:

```
public override House CreateHouse()
{
    return new HUDHouse();
}
```

The `CreateFloor()` method creates a new class of type `SlabFloor`:

```
public override Floor CreateFloor()
{
    return new SlabFloor();
}
```

The `CreateWall()` method creates a new class of type `WoodenWall`:

```
public override Wall CreateWall()
{
    return new WoodenWall();
}
```

The `CreateRoof()` method creates a new class of type `ShingledRoof`:

```
public override Roof CreateRoof()
{
    return new ShingledRoof();
}
}
```

The last step is to refactor the builder to accept the abstract factory class as an input parameter of the `Build()` method instead of declaring `DuplexFactory` inside the builder. Notice that the internal code of the builder did not need to change much. We simply changed the `Build()` method to have an input parameter `HouseFactory`. Now we can change the type of house we build by simply entering the correct implementation of `HouseFactory`. This allows a polymorphic integration between factory types without complicating the builder any more than is needed or changing the builder for each house type.

```
public class HouseBuilder
{
    public House Build(HouseFactory factory)
    {
        House house = factory.CreateHouse();
        house.Floor = factory.CreateFloor();
        house.WestWall = factory.CreateWall();
        house.EastWall = factory.CreateWall();
        house.SouthWall = factory.CreateWall();
        house.NorthWall = factory.CreateWall();
        house.Roof = factory.CreateRoof();
        return house;
    }

}
```

We now can change how the builder works by simply passing in a new factory instance of type `HouseFactory`. We get a new type of `House` depending on which factory the builder gets as its input parameter:

```
HouseBuilder builder = new HouseBuilder();
House duplex = builder.Build(new DuplexFactory());
House hud = builder.Build(new HUDFactory());
```

When we look at the results of our test for this code, we can see that each type has its expected implementations:

```
Duplex:
--Floor: CementFloor
--WestWall: CementBlockWall
--EastWall: CementBlockWall
--SouthWall: CementBlockWall
--NorthWall: CementBlockWall
```

```
--Roof: ShingledRoof
HUDHouse:
--Floor: SlabFloor
--WestWall: WoodenWall
--EastWall: WoodenWall
--SouthWall: WoodenWall
--NorthWall: WoodenWall
--Roof: ShingledRoof
```

Comparison to Similar Patterns

Abstract Factories are an abstraction of factory implementation, so whether to use a Factory or abstract the factory depends on your need. It may make more sense to use different factories inside a Builder or pass the factory into a Builder as an abstract one. Builders that accept Abstract Factories sometimes work better than Builders that accept one single factory type. Another option to the Abstract Factory is using a Builder with a director. The director accepts different builder types with operational methods and deals with each operational method in turn. This might be more useful if you have to implement several operations in the creational process instead of one. Factories usually are more useful with a specific class type or series of class types all subclassed from a single base. Abstract Factories are simply an expanded version of the Factory pattern, where the Factory needs to have a polymorphic implementation.

What We Have Learned

In the solutions we saw how to take different factories for classes with a common base, provide polymorphic cohesion between these class's factories using the Abstract Factory pattern, and in effect simplify and/or enhance the overall code. We used this pattern to define a contract or common interface between factories used by similar objects, and using this contract allowed the base class to handle the actual factory call. We also learned a valuable lesson on polymorphism that incorporates similarities in interfaces between classes and, depending on the implementations of those classes, causes different actions to be performed. We found another positive aspect of polymorphism, in that it can enhance the maintainability of your code with respect to the way the factory implementation is used instead of having different multiple conditional logic areas either in classes or builders.

Related Patterns

- Builder pattern
- Factory pattern
- Template pattern

Builder Pattern

What Is a Builder Pattern?

Builders are a type of creational pattern that consolidates code for initialization and configuration of objects. Usually builders house several operations that may be involved in the creational processes involved in building classes, and often work hand in hand with factories. Builders usually deal with construction of complex objects or objects whose construction, initialization, and configuration spans more than one process and whose creational code is complex.

Builders are used to prevent duplication of creational code, and act as a central repository for the creational code involved. So a builder might be used when you have several processes that aid in the creation of an object, and the object's creation or initialization is dependent on each of these processes. You might use different factories as input parameters for a builder, changing the way a builder constructs its object, or the type of object it constructs. Or you might use the builder inside or alongside a factory to aid the factory's creation of its objects.

The Builder pattern has three main components: the *Builder*, the *Director*, and the *Product*. The builder is responsible for defining and producing individual parts of a whole class or product. It holds a number of processes needed to build, initialize, and configure the product class. The director class is the class that helps the builder to put all the methods together in a cohesive and consequential manner. When used with factories, directors can actually be the

builder themselves. The product is the class that is pro-
duced from the builder-director relationship.

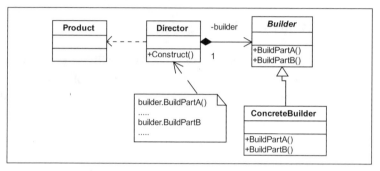

Figure 2-8. UML for Builder pattern

Problem 1: A class needs several operations to create and initialize each of its attributes in an expected order of operations, and each class type instance needs different attribute values

For our real-world example, let's assume we have a class
that uses several operations to get its fully configured and
initialized created state. We will use the same House class
we used in the "Abstract Factory Pattern" section in this
chapter to illustrate our problem.

Below we have the creational code for House. Notice we
are first creating the House class, then initializing each of
its attributes with different classes. For this example, we
can assume each attribute type has a base parent class from
which the implementation class for the attribute is inherited. We can also assume that each attribute needs to be
created and added to the House class in a set order of
operations and each attribute must be set before the class

can be considered as fully configured and initialized from the code.

```
House house = new Duplex();
house.Floor = new SlabFloor();
house.WestWall = new CementWall();
house.EastWall = new CementWall();
house.SouthWall = new CementWall();
house.NorthWall = new CementWall();
house.Roof = new ShingledRoof();
```

Our problem is that we are using specialized code to create and initialize the Duplex class. If we wanted to create and configure another House class type and have all its attributes set up in the same order as the Duplex class, we would have to create a different set of functional logic:

```
House house = new HUDHouse();
house.Floor = new CementFloor();
house.WestWall = new CementBlockWall();
house.EastWall = new CementBlockWall();
house.SouthWall = new CementBlockWall();
house.NorthWall = new CementBlockWall();
house.Roof = new ShingledRoof();
```

This duplicate logic might introduce uniformity and maintenance issues across the different creational logic areas. We would then have multiple areas to maintain and keep uniform, for exactly the same operational order and set of operations.

Solution 1: Use a combination of a director and a builder to encapsulate and uniformly define the processes in the expected order, and use inherited members of the builder to change each type's reaction to the expected operations

The first step in figuring out the solution is to realize we have a set of operations that need to maintain a certain order for every class implementation of House. We also need to make sure that each operation gets performed before the House class can be returned from the code.

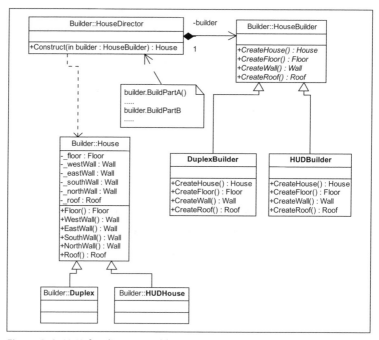

Figure 2-9. UML for director Builder pattern example

To accomplish this we will use the Builder pattern. We first need to create a common interface for the concrete builder classes. We use an abstract class with abstract methods that each concrete builder class will implement. The abstract `HouseBuilder` class is used for this. We inherit each class of type `HouseBuilder` from the abstraction and implement each method in a different way depending on the type of `House` we want the builder to build. Notice each abstract method in the class is a method we took from our original code. The only thing missing is the order in which each is called and the actual implementation of the methods.

Creational Patterns

```
public abstract class HouseBuilder
{
    public abstract House CreateHouse();
    public abstract Floor CreateFloor();
    public abstract Wall CreateWall();
    public abstract Roof CreateRoof();

}
```

For this example we created two builders, `Duplex` and `HUDHouse,` for `House` classes:

```
class DuplexBuilder : HouseBuilder
{
    public override House CreateHouse()
    {
        return new Duplex();
    }
    public override Floor CreateFloor()
    {
        return new CementFloor();
    }
    public override Wall CreateWall()
    {
        return new CementBlockWall();
```

```
    }
    public override Roof CreateRoof()
    {
        return new ShingledRoof();
    }
}
```

Each of these concrete classes implements the
`HouseBuilder`'s abstract methods, and each method
works in a different manner for its different concrete
implementations:

```
class HUDBuilder : HouseBuilder
{
    public override House CreateHouse()
    {
        return new HUDHouse();
    }
    public override Floor CreateFloor()
    {
        return new SlabFloor();
    }
    public override Wall CreateWall()
    {
        return new WoodenWall();
    }
    public override Roof CreateRoof()
    {
        return new ShingledRoof();
    }
}
```

Now that we have builders that implement each of the
creational methods for its house type, we need a way to
make sure we perform the same order of operations for any
builder. For this purpose we create a `Director` class that
has a method that receives as an input parameter the
abstract `HouseBuilder` class. Inside the director class's

`Construct()` method we identify each operation and its order of execution. This ensures that no matter which `House` class we want to create we always configure them in a uniform manner. Doing this provides us with an easily maintainable area for making additions and modifications to the order of operations, and ensures we always get expected results from our creational methods.

```
class HouseDirector
{
    public House Construct(HouseBuilder builder)
    {
        House house = builder.CreateHouse();
        house.Floor = builder.CreateFloor();
        house.EastWall = builder.CreateWall();
        house.WestWall = builder.CreateWall();
        house.SouthWall = builder.CreateWall();
        house.NorthWall = builder.CreateWall();
        house.Roof = builder.CreateRoof();
        return house;
    }
}
```

Now we have a way of using our builder classes to create and configure the type of `House` class we need while maintaining a uniform order of operations. The `HouseDirector` class maintains the order of the operations and the builder implementation classes return the correct classes and attributes appropriate for their type:

```
HouseDirector director = new HouseDirector();
House duplex = director.Construct(new DuplexBuilder());
House hud = director.Construct(new HUDBuilder());
```

We now have captured both the workflow and each separate implementation of that workflow in a central location. This adds to the maintainability of the code and establishes a pattern for future additions or revisions. When we run the test for this code we see each `House` type renders its expected attributes:

```
Create a Duplex:
--Floor: CementFloor
--WestWall: CementBlockWall
--EastWall: CementBlockWall
--SouthWall: CementBlockWall
--NorthWall: CementBlockWall
--Roof: ShingledRoof
```

And here we can see how a different implementation type will render a different instance of type `House`:

```
Create a HUDHouse:
--Floor: SlabFloor
--WestWall: WoodenWall
--EastWall: WoodenWall
--SouthWall: WoodenWall
--NorthWall: WoodenWall
--Roof: ShingledRoof
```

Problem 2: A factory produces classes that need initialization, configuration, data, or state set during creation and this can differ between class types and spans multiple operations

Let's look at the suit example from the "Factory Pattern" section earlier in this chapter. Remember that we had an abstract parent class `Suit` that we inherited from to get different implementation subclasses of that class. Now assume that our `Suit` subclasses are part of an entire ensemble, and the `Suit` attributes need to be initialized and configured when the implementation class of `Suit` is created from the factory to include the ensemble variations. Some of these attributes are part of the `Suit` abstraction, some are only valid for individual inherited implementations of `Suit`, and each attribute object is subclassed from a common abstraction class. We need within our factory to completely initialize all the attributes for the particular implementation. For reasons of maintainability and scalability we do not wish to use the current Boolean logic code we have created for that purpose.

```
....resides inside the factory
if(suitType == SuitType.Armani)
{
    suit = new Armani();
    suit.Tie = new StripedTie();
    suit.Belt = new LeatherBelt();
    suit.CuffLinks = new GoldCuffLinks();
}
```

If we had to create different suits in different places at different times, and add different pieces of the ensemble to get the correct combination, the code would have to be duplicated, which would be a maintenance issue:

```
....resides inside the factory after Armani
    suit.CuffLinks = new GoldCuffLinks();
}
else if(suitType == SuitType.PlaidBusinessSuit)
{
    suit = new PlaidBusinessSuit();
    suit.Tie = null;
    suit.Belt = null;
}
```

Also, we have no way to determine in a standard way which pieces of the ensemble should be added to the suit. Each different type has different accessories that must be initialized in different ways, as we can see in the example above. We do not have a seamless way to add this functionality into the factory at this time.

Solution 2: Use registered builders for each class type inside your factory to aid in the initialization of class types

To allow us to configure each ensemble type by the suit type, we need to make use of a creational pattern type: the Builder. A builder basically is a class that encapsulates several initialization, configuration, or data access operations for building a class type. So, for a particular group of inherited members of Suit, we will need a different builder to configure each type's attributes in different ways.

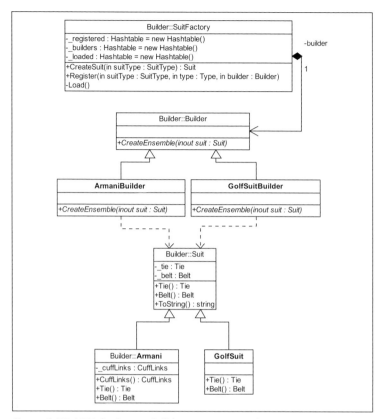

Figure 2-10. UML for factory Builder pattern example

Below we see the code for the Suit object:

```
public abstract class Suit
{
    Tie _tie;
    Belt _belt;
```

We have added two properties, which give us extended functionality. These properties will need to be configured on creation of the inherited members.

```
    public Tie Tie
    {
        get{return _tie;}
        set{_tie = value;}
    }
    public Belt Belt
    {
        get{return _belt;}
        set{_belt = value;}
    }

}
```

Here we have the concrete implementations of `Suit`. Notice that only the Armani suit has extended properties for this example.

```
public class Armani : Suit
{
    CuffLinks _cuffLinks;
    public CuffLinks CuffLinks
    {
        get{return _cuffLinks;}
        set{_cuffLinks = value;}
    }
}
public class StripedBusinessSuit : Suit
{

}
public class PlaidBusinessSuit : Suit
{

}
public class GolfSuit : Suit
{

}
```

Now we need to create an individual builder for each type of Suit we wish to configure. To accomplish this in a uniform fashion and to provide a uniform interface between builders for implementations inside the factory, we need to establish an abstract base class for the builder with a common abstract method. We will name this class simply Builder. The abstract method we will call Create-Ensemble(). This method is implemented in the inherited builder members, and will perform their specialized configuration of the Suit implementation class.

```
public abstract class Builder
{
    public abstract void CreateEnsemble(ref Suit suit);
}
```

Notice below in the GolfSuitBuilder class example that inside this specialized builder's CreateEnsemble() method we define the expected type of Suit to be configured inside the builder. This is important because, based on the different inherited members, we have extended attributes to set as well as different values for attributes common to the parent class.

```
public class GolfSuitBuilder : Builder
{
    public override void CreateEnsemble(ref Suit suit)
    {
        GolfSuit aSuit = (GolfSuit)suit;
        aSuit.Tie = null;
        aSuit.Belt = new LeatherBelt();
    }

}
```

Creational Patterns (side margin)

In the `ArmaniBuilder` concrete builder we define the extended attribute in the `Armani` suit class we defined previously as `CuffLinks`:

```
public class ArmaniBuilder : Builder
{
    public override void CreateEnsemble(ref Suit suit)
    {
        Armani aSuit = (Armani)suit;
        aSuit.Tie = new StripedTie();
        aSuit.Belt = new LeatherBelt();
        aSuit.CuffLinks = new GoldCuffLinks();
            //extended attribute for Armani

    }

}
```

Creating a builder in this fashion ties the builder indirectly to a particular type of suit.

Now we need to create our factory class. We define which type of suit we can render from the factory by adding the builder as a parameter in the factory's `Register()` method. We use as a key for this method the enum `SuitType`. This defines within our factory at run time the particular builder class we wish to associate with an instance of `Suit`.

```
public sealed class SuitFactory
{
    ...
    public void Register(SuitType suitType, Type type,
                         Builder builder)
    {
        _registered.Add(suitType,type);
        _builders.Add(suitType,builder);
    }
```

Our `CreateSuit()` method on the factory works the same as it did in the Factory pattern example we read about earlier, with one difference:

```
public Suit CreateSuit(SuitType suitType)
{
    if(_loaded[suitType] == null)
        Load();
    Suit suit = (Suit)_loaded[suitType];
```

Instead of just returning a simple `Suit` class, we are now configuring within the factory the attributes of each concrete implementation using our registered builder. After we get our concrete instance of the `Suit` class, we pass it into the appropriate builder (if one is present) to be initialized:

```
    if(_builders[suitType] != null)
    {
        Builder builder = (Builder)_builders[suitType];
        builder.CreateEnsemble(ref suit);
    }
    return suit;
    }
}
```

Notice how the director role is spread in this example between the factory and builder. The builder defines some operations; the factory decides which builder to associate with which class in the factory. This is an example of how the director role can be very flexible in regard to its actual implementation.

Now when we define our expected types of `Suit` in our code, we also define the expected builder. This allows us to change the builder for each class type, or not have one at all if we choose, enabling a wide host of specialized configuration options.

```
SuitFactory factory = new SuitFactory();
factory.Register(SuitType.Armani, typeof(Armani),
                new ArmaniBuilder());
factory.Register(SuitType.GolfSuit, typeof(GolfSuit),
                new GolfSuitBuilder());
factory.Register(SuitType.PlaidBusinessSuit, typeof
                (PlaidBusinessSuit), null);
factory.Register(SuitType.StripedBusinessSuit, typeof
                (StripedBusinessSuit), null);
```

When we create our concrete implementation of `Suit` we get back an instance of a fully configured class. The manner in which each property is configured depends on its type of class and builder.

```
Suit suit = factory.CreateSuit(SuitType.Armani);
suit = factory.CreateSuit(SuitType.GolfSuit);
suit = factory.CreateSuit(SuitType.PlaidBusinessSuit);
suit = factory.CreateSuit(SuitType.StripedBusinessSuit);
```

When running our test we see that for each type we call from our factory we get back a specialized concrete instance. If there are extended attributes, those are set. Each attribute is set up according to its particular builder's order of operations and initialized in the proper manner dependent on the builder.

```
Armani{StripedTie, LeatherBelt} extended:{GoldCuffLinks}
GolfSuit{No Tie, LeatherBelt}
PlaidBusinessSuit{No Tie, No Belt}
StripedBusinessSuit{No Tie, No Belt}
```

Comparison to Similar Patterns

Builders are useful when dealing with multiple operational methods. They do not necessarily create a series of classes. Factories are better suited to handle this particular problem. As you saw in the examples, Builders and Factories can usually work hand in hand either with a Factory inside a Builder, vice versa, or side by side. Abstract Factories are sometimes useful when you want different factories to act on the Builder in different ways.

What We Have Learned

Builders are useful for any creational methods spanning a number of operations. They are also useful for maintaining the order of the operations in creating classes. Using inheritance, we can make sure builders can provide us polymorphic processing of creational logic and can change this logic across inherited implementations. Using builders we can create a class, initialize its state, and maintain the order of operations for how the class gets created and configured. We can use builders in a variety of ways with factories and provide either added functionality or enhanced usability in their association.

Related Patterns

- Abstract Factory pattern
- Factory pattern
- Template pattern

Prototype Pattern

What Is a Prototype Pattern?

The *Prototype* pattern gives us a way to deal with creating new instances of objects from existing object instances. We basically produce a copy or *clone* of a class that we already have created and configured. This allows us to capture the present state of the original object in its clone so we can modify the cloned object without introducing those changes to the original. We might do this if we needed to duplicate a class for some reason but creating a new class was not appropriate.

Perhaps the class we wanted to clone had a particular internal state we wanted to duplicate. Creating a new class from scratch would not reproduce the appropriate internal variable values in the new class we desired without violating rules of encapsulation of the class. This might occur because we might not be able to directly access private variables inside the class. Simply constructing a new class would not get us the class in its current state. Making a clone of the existing class would allow the clone to be modified and used without changing the original and would allow us to capture the originating class's state in the new class. This can be accomplished because the prototype method is internal to the originating class, and has access to its class's internal variables. This gives the method direct access to both the originating and the new class's internal state.

Another reason to use a prototype would be because we cannot create a new class in the current scope of the code or because allowing a constructor on the class in the current scope violates the rules of encapsulation of our application. A situation like this could occur if the class's constructor was marked internal to a domain that is not the current domain. We could not call the constructor because of its encapsulation properties. This sometimes happens in cases where a facade is used. Since you cannot call the constructor outside of the facade's domain, the only way to construct a new instance of a class would be to provide a prototype method on the class.

The Prototype pattern has one main component: the *Prototype*. The prototype is really an ordinary class that has a method implemented to create a copy (or clone) of itself.

This is an interesting and useful pattern. Let's take a look at some examples of how it can be used.

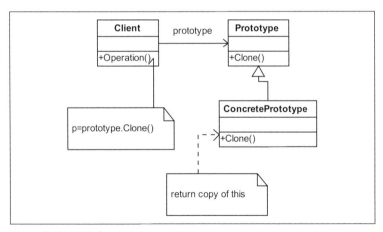

Figure 2-11. UML for Prototype pattern

Problem: A class that cannot be constructed outside its assembly or package needs a copy made that keeps its current state intact

For our example, we start with a class that can only be constructed internally to an assembly or package. We need to create a new instance of the class in a scope that is outside of the assembly or package of the class. Since the constructor is marked internal to its domain, assembly, or package, we cannot call it in the current scope.

The `Stone` class needs to be added to another class outside its package or assembly without sharing the current reference. The only way to do that is to call the factory method again and get a new instance. This might be inappropriate since the `Stone` class may have changed attributes that we wish to maintain in the new class. We have tried to fix this problem by creating a new class and filling its attributes with the values of the original:

```
Stone stone = StoneFactory.GetGranite();
stone.Color = System.Drawing.Color.DimGray;
stone.Hardness = 5;
stone.Shape = System.Drawing.Drawing2D.WarpMode.Bilinear;
```

Calling the factory to get a new class will give us a new instance, but we have to be careful to write the code so we can get an exact replica of the original:

```
Stone nonClonedStone = StoneFactory.GetGranite();
nonClonedStone.Color = stone.Color;
nonClonedStone.Hardness = stone.Hardness;
nonClonedStone.Shape = stone.Shape;
```

This will only work as long as we can set the internal variables of the class through methods providing external access to these variables. If we had attributes that we could not set inside the new class, this method would not work. Our problem is that we *do* have such variables; we just cannot modify the internal state of the class easily from outside the class. We need a way to get a new instance of the class with its complete state maintained in the new class.

Solution: Create a prototype method on the class to return a cloned instance with its state copied to the needed depth

Our solution to this dilemma is to build a method on the class that will produce a prototype of the original. In other words, we clone or copy the class with a method that has internal access to the class without violating the class's encapsulation rules.

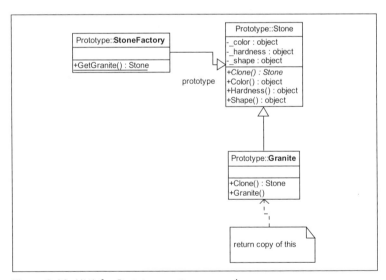

Figure 2-12. UML for Prototype pattern example

We start by looking at the abstract `Stone` class. We provide an abstract method on the class named `Clone()`. This method will be implemented on the concrete implementations of the class to provide a way to return the particular instance of the class with its current state at the time of the call to the method.

```
abstract class Stone
{
    public abstract Stone Clone();
}
```

Now let's look at the implementation class `Granite` and its `Clone()` method. We use the .NET `MemberwiseClone()` method to render a *shallow copy* of the attributes of the class in its current state:

```
class Granite : Stone
{
    public override Stone Clone()
    {
        return (Granite)this.MemberwiseClone();
    }
}
```

In the case of having data that lived deeper in the object, we might have to capture the internal state directly. This could occur, for instance, in an object containing collections of object instances, and the collections would not necessarily get cloned because the objects in them were reference types instead of value types. In this case, you might have to add each object manually. This is referred to as a *deep copy*. A deep copy occurs when you have copied new reference types from existing ones, in addition to using `MemberwiseClone()` to copy the value types, making a completely disconnected new class instance. This results in an object whose internal reference types are not shared but are new instances of the original reference types. This ensures changes to the cloned object's reference types do not affect the object from which it was cloned. In the following example, we are copying all the value types from the current object to a new object, then looping through the current object's internal collection and calling a clone object on the value type in the collection:

```
public override Stone Clone()
{
    Stone ret = (Granite)this.MemberwiseClone();
    foreach(object obj in _collection)
        ret.Add(obj.Clone()); //Reference Type is also cloned
    return ret;
}
```

Now when we call the method it produces an exact copy with the same internal state as the original class:

```
Stone clonedStone = stone.Clone();
```

Our test of the new class confirms this:

```
Cloned
Color:Color [DimGray]
Hardness:5
Shape:Bilinear
```

Comparison to Similar Patterns

Depending on the scope and purpose of the creational methods, either a Factory or a Singleton pattern might be a better solution than the Prototype pattern. If you need a global instance of a class that cannot be instanced more than once, then a Singleton might be more appropriate. A Factory might also be another option for a more global management site for the object's state. The Factory could retain created objects and their states, and render them as needed.

What We Have Learned

The Prototype pattern gives us another way to deal with creating a class when copying the original object's state is important. It is also useful when the object cannot be created in its current context without violating the object's encapsulation rules. The pattern basically provides a clone of the original object, maintaining all of the original object's current state.

Related Patterns

- Factory pattern
- Singleton pattern
- Template pattern

Singleton Pattern

What Is a Singleton Pattern?

The *Singleton* pattern is a way to provide global access to a class instance without making the constructor available outside the class. The singleton class instantiates itself and maintains that instance across multiple process threads.

The Singleton pattern has one main component: the *Singleton*. The singleton class acts as a global repository for an instance of itself, whose constructor is private. So no instance outside the class can be created, and only one instance resides inside the singleton.

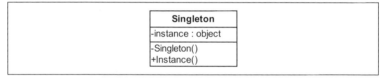

Figure 2-13. UML for Singleton pattern

If, for example, we had a main *MDI* (*multiple document interface*) window for an application and wanted only one instance of this window, but wanted to allow many different process threads to access this one instance and maintain the state of the MDI window between the different calls, we might use a singleton.

Problem: A global class in the application needs to hide its constructor and maintain only one instance of itself while allowing all of its methods to be accessed as instance methods

For our example, we have a class that we wish to have globally accessible in our application. We want to allow only one instance of that class to exist. For purposes of state management, we need a class instance to be provided for each method on the class instead of making the methods *static* (shared between threads). We do not wish more than one instance of the class to be created.

In our present code, the state of our MDI class cannot be maintained across multiple threads. This class is called `MDIWindow` and has a public constructor. The class can be instanced any number of times.

```
class MDIWindow
{
    public State StateOf
    {
        get{return _state;}
        set{_state = value;}
    }

    public void Init()
    {
        ...Some code here
    }
}
```

Obviously, maintaining state across multiple process threads is not possible with this model, as we can see in the following code. The class is instanced only in the current process thread.

```
MDIWindow nonSingleton = new MDIWindow();
nonSingleton.StateOf = State.New;
nonSingleton.Init();
nonSingleton.StateOf = State.Initialized;
```

Another process thread has to create a new instance:

```
MDIWindow nonSingleton = new MDIWindow();
. . . . . . . .
```

Solution: Use the Singleton pattern to hide the constructor and maintain an instance of the class inside itself

We have to maintain the state of our class across multiple instances while keeping its scope global. To accomplish this, we will use the Singleton pattern to hide the constructor of the class and provide an instance. The actual constructor of the class needs to be hidden and the class instance needs to be internal to the class itself, limiting the number of instances to one static or global instance.

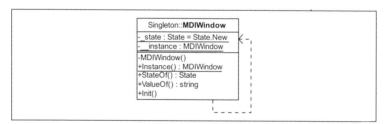

Figure 2-14. UML for Singleton pattern example

The first step to creating our singleton is to make the constructor private. This allows only the class itself to have access to its creation.

```
class MDIWindow
{
    private MDIWindow()
    {
        //... no-op for a singleton
    }
```

Next, we need to provide a method that will create the single internal instance of the class. We call this method for this example `Instance`. We use this method to initialize the class if not already done and to access the single instance.

```
//Lazy creation of singleton internal instance
    public static MDIWindow Instance
    {
        get
        {
            lock(typeof(MDIWindow))
            {
                if(_instance == null)
                    _instance = new MDIWindow();
            }
            return _instance;
        }
    }
```

Notice that the `Instance` method is marked `static`. This is done to allow all threads consistent access. To control multi-threaded access we use the `lock` statement outside the instance creation. This allows us to lock the instance creation to a single thread (the first one). This is important to keep multiple threads from creating their own instance before the first thread gets through the code. All the following process threads after the first one will see a non-null instance of our `MDIWindow` class and not try to create it again.

> **Note**   The `lock` keyword from .NET used in the example above is needed to keep multiple threads from accessing the code within the statement at the same time. It keeps the access to the code block concurrent and synchronized. Java uses the `synchronized` keyword to perform the same functionality.

Another way to do this is to use a mutex or a semaphore. A *mutex* is a thread synchronization device that allows access to only one thread.

```
private static Mutex mutex;
......
    if (mutex == null)
            mutex = new Mutex();
```

By using a mutex in your code you can restrict access to all other threads at a certain point and make them wait. In the case of the C# example below, the `WaitOne()` method sets the first accessing thread as the blocking thread:

```
mutex.WaitOne();
```

This allows a single thread to process the null check for the instance variable, much like it is done using the `lock` keyword:

```
if(_instance == null)
    _instance = new MDIWindow();
```

Only after you release the mutex from the thread can these other threads have access to the mutex. This ensures that you do not have multiple threads trying to create a single instance over and over in a disorganized fashion.

```
    mutex.ReleaseMutex();
}
```

The difference between a mutex and a *semaphore* is that a mutex enforces thread identity, and the semaphore does not.

All the other methods in the class are non-static public methods. These are the methods that will be accessible on the internal instance of the class.

```
public State StateOf
{
    get{return _state;}
}
public string ValueOf
{
    set
    {
        if(_state == State.Initialized)
            _state = State.Runnable;
        else if(_state == State.Runnable)
            _state = State.Modified;
    }
}
public void Init()
    {
    if(_state == State.New)
        _state = State.Initialized;
}
```

When we look at the code to access the MDIWindow class, we see that any access to the class instance is done through the Instance method. All the public methods are available in this manner. The constructor is not accessible, guaranteeing that all threads use the same instance of the object. And since we used a thread locking method, we are guaranteed of only one instance being created even if multiple threads are accessing the `Instance` method for the first time.

To test this we can call code on different threads to modify the state of the singleton class as shown below. First, we create an array of threads that we will use to access our singleton class:

```
Thread[] stateLessThreads = new Thread[_numberOfThreads];

TestRun entry1 = new TestRun();
TestRun entry2 = new TestRun();
TestRun entry3 = new TestRun();
```

Next, we start each thread:

```
Thread t = new Thread(new ThreadStart(entry1.StateThread));
stateLessThreads[0] = t;

t = new Thread(new ThreadStart(entry2.StateThread));
stateLessThreads[1] = t;

t = new Thread(new ThreadStart(entry3.StateThread));
stateLessThreads[2] = t;
```

The order in which each thread will execute our singleton code is arbitrary; there is no guarantee as to the order of entry of any thread:

```
for (int i = 0; i < _3; i++) stateLessThreads[i].Start();
```

When the first thread calls the `Instance` property method, it locks the singleton creation code from being accessed by any other threads. It doesn't matter which thread gets there first. None of the other threads can get past that code until it has finished and the locking mechanism has been released.

```
public void StateThread()
{
    MDIWindow.Instance.Init();
    MDIWindow.Instance.ValueOf = "changed";
    MDIWindow.Instance.StateOf);
}
```

The test above will show that state is maintained for the single instance across all threads. The first thread changes the status to New, then to Initialized, and last to Runnable by modifying a value that changes our state accessor. The next thread sees the new status of Runnable, and changes it to Modified. The last thread to access the singleton sees the new status of Modified and, since this status does not change, the thread leaves the status as is.

```
Thread{3} Singleton state before Init call:New
Thread{3} Singleton state after Init call:Initialized
Thread{3} Singleton state after Value change:Runnable
Thread{1} Singleton state after Init call:Runnable
Thread{1} Singleton state after Value change:Modified
Thread{2} Singleton state after Init call:Modified
Thread{2} Singleton state after Value change:Modified
```

Comparison to Similar Patterns

To control access to the constructor of a class, especially when you don't wish to allow the constructor to be accessed outside a package or namespace, Singletons and Prototypes both work well. It all depends on how you wish to deal with the scope of the instance. Since the Prototype hides the creational method inside the Clone() method, obviously your constructor is safe from outside access. A Singleton pattern works the same way, but only allows one instance instead of many cloned instances.

What We Have Learned

Using the Singleton pattern allows us to control the construction access of a global class instance. We can use it to provide singular class instance access when we do not want to allow multiple instances and want the class itself to control its scope.

The Singleton pattern is the first pattern I ever learned to use. I used this pattern most extensively for creating classes for holding code to perform database select queries. It is a handy way for you to control and limit the scope of any class that you do not want to create over and over. Just be careful. This pattern can be addictive and you may end up using it when it is not appropriate when you first start using patterns.

Related Patterns

- Observer pattern
- Prototype pattern
- State pattern

3

Behavioral Patterns

Behavioral patterns are patterns whose sole purpose is to facilitate the work of algorithmic calculations and communication between classes. They use inheritance heavily to control code flow. They define and produce process and run-time flow and identify hierarchies of classes and when and where they become instantiated in code. Some define class instance and state, some hand off work from one class to another, and some provide placeholders for other functionality.

Chain of Responsibility Pattern

What Is a Chain of Responsibility Pattern?

The *Chain of Responsibility* pattern performs a lot like it sounds. If you have a group of classes that are all interdependent on each other and each performs a particular piece of processing, this pattern is a very useful tool. It makes sure each member in a chain controls when and to what class it hands its processing to. The pattern controls the code flow by using inheritance and by allowing instances of its predecessors to be loaded one inside the other, forming in effect a chain of classes that hand off to the next class in the chain at the end of its turn.

The Chain of Responsibility pattern has a single main component: the *Handler*. The handler object encapsulates the entire chain of handler instances inside each other instance. In other words, the first link in the chain contains the next and that link contains each consecutive link. As you move through each link's process and that process finishes, it automatically checks for the existence of the next consecutive link and calls the process of that next link. This can happen no matter which level of link in the chain you call and will continue down the chain until the chain ends.

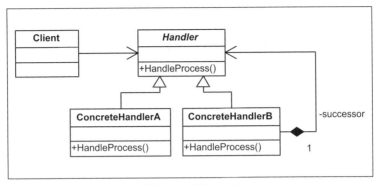

Figure 3-1. UML for Chain of Responsibility pattern

Problem: A group of classes each have processes to run in turn, but there is no way to directly determine in which class order each should run its process

For our example, we have a group of classes with a common parent. The parent class has a *virtual* method, Run(), which performs the actual process run on each class. Right now we have no cohesion between these classes and no way to guarantee how each class will access its Run() method or in which order. We need a way to define the order of operations between each of the classes, and define class responsibilities in the process flow.

```
Process firstProcess = new FirstProcess();
firstProcess.Run();
Process secondProcess = new SecondProcess();
secondProcess.Run();
Process thirdProcess = new ThirdProcess();
thirdProcess.Run();
```

Behavioral Patterns

Solution: Use a chained association of classes that have interdependence on each other to define the order of operations

In the problem above we stated we had no apparent order in which to run our class methods. We could call each in turn in code, but we need to encapsulate the execution of the method and call the next class's method inside each class. After each class executes its Run() method, it should call the next class in a chained fashion.

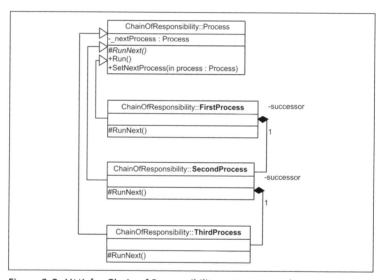

Figure 3-2. UML for Chain of Responsibility pattern example

Using a Chain of Responsibility pattern, we pull the class execution responsibility into the class itself, allowing each class to contain an instance of the next class in its chain. To facilitate this process we add a new abstract method to the abstract base class Process. This method, RunNext(), contains the implementation code that we originally had in the Run() method. We make it protected to hide it from access outside the class and to allow the `Run()` method to act as the gate for each consecutive method.

```
abstract class Process
{
```

We have an instance variable in each of the chained classes that holds the instance for the next class:

```
private Process _nextProcess;
```

Our concrete implementations will handle how the current step in the chain gets called:

```
protected abstract void RunNext();
```

The `Run()` method is the way in which we start the chain at a certain point. We first call the `RunNext()` method to start the chain processing on the current class. Next, we check to see if there is another process in the chain. If so, we run that, passing control down into that class.

```
public void Run()
{
    RunNext();
    if(_nextProcess != null)
    {
        _nextProcess.Run();
    }
}
```

This chain of actions continues as long as there is a class instance of the next chained class inside the executing class.

The class also has a public method to allow the setting up of the next process to be called. This should be done at class initialization time before the `Run()` method is called:

```
public void SetNextProcess(Process process)
{
    _nextProcess = process;
```

Behavioral Patterns

```
    }
}
```

Below we see the code for each concrete class implementation. Notice each class has a different process that it performs. For this example, we just pause the thread for a different time period:

```
class FirstProcess : Process
{
    protected override void RunNext()
    {
        System.Threading.Thread.Sleep(1000);
    }
}

class SecondProcess : Process
{
    protected override void RunNext()
    {
        System.Threading.Thread.Sleep(2000);
    }
}

class ThirdProcess : Process
{
    protected override void RunNext()
    {
        System.Threading.Thread.Sleep(3000);
    }
}
```

To set up the chain we use a method to include the class instances inside each other: SetNextProcess(). This method in effect registers one class inside another class, identifying the sequence of processes to execute.

```
Process firstProcess = new FirstProcess();
Process secondProcess = new SecondProcess();
```

```
Process thirdProcess = new ThirdProcess();
firstProcess.SetNextProcess(secondProcess);
secondProcess.SetNextProcess(thirdProcess);
thirdProcess.SetNextProcess(null);
```

Calling the `Run()` method on any of the process instances will in turn call its next instance in the chain on to the last registered instance:

```
firstProcess.Run ();
```

Any of the classes in the sequence can then be called, and all of the classes contained in it will execute in turn down through the chain. Here we see output if we start running our process on the first class:

```
Beginning first process....
Ending first process....
Beginning second process....
Ending second process....
Beginning third process....
Ending third process....
```

Comparison to Similar Patterns

Depending on whether you wish to provide a set operational cycle or you want to change that cycle on the fly might influence your decision to use the Chain of Responsibility pattern or a Command pattern. The Command pattern holds an order of operations in its command queue, but allows ad-hoc calls to any operation desired via the command object. In contrast, the Chain of Responsibility pattern more rigidly defines the order of operations. Your particular usage depends on which is more suitable to your needs. The Chain of Responsibility also is like the Composite pattern in that parsing through the class chain is like moving through each collection class in the composite. Both patterns move through class methods in a serial fashion.

What We Have Learned

The Chain of Responsibility pattern seems to be quite a good way to link classes that have interdependence on each other in an order of operations. You could implement the pattern in an approval cycle, where people needed to approve specific requests in turn. You could use it to determine an order of operations for executing nearly any kind of code. This order can easily be changed at run time or in different code instances, depending on the need.

Related Patterns

- Command pattern
- Composite pattern
- Template pattern

Command Pattern

What Is a Command Pattern?

A *Command* pattern allows requests to an object to exist as objects. What does that mean? It means that if you send a request for some function to an object, the command object can house that request inside the object. This is useful in the case of undoing or redoing some action, or simply storing an action in a request queue on an object. When you send the request, it is stored in the object. Then later if you need to access that same request or apply the request or some method on the request to an object, you can use the request object instead of calling the object's method directly.

The Command pattern has three main components: the *Invoker*, the *Command*, and the *Receiver*. The invoker component acts as a link between the commands and the receiver and houses the receiver and the individual

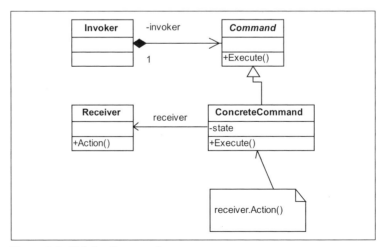

Figure 3-3. UML for Command pattern

Behavioral Patterns

commands as they are sent. The command is an object that encapsulates a request to the receiver. The receiver is the component that is acted upon by each request.

Let's take a look at an example of this interesting pattern. The example demonstrates a way to perform changes and undo those changes to text in a document. It shows how to use the command as a request to add some words to the document and store that text request.

Problem: A document object needs a way to add and store undo and redo actions

For our example, we will take a typical problem you may have encountered when using a simple text application like Notepad. You add some text, then find you need to undo what you have added. Sometime later you realize you actually wanted the text after all, and wish to add it back to the document. Most of the simple text applications available don't have an undo queue or have one for only one action. In the example below, there is no such functionality. You realize that this would be a really useful feature to add, since your document has no concept of history of changes made to its text. Your current `Document` object stores text as lines of strings within an `ArrayList`. When you remove the text, it is gone, with no way to redo your previous text.

```
//receiver
class Document
{
```

A collection object stores each line of text:

```
    private ArrayList _textArray = new ArrayList();
```

Methods exist for adding and removing lines of text. When text is added or removed, it is permanent; you cannot get it back if removed.

```
public void Write(string text)
{
    _textArray.Add(text);
}
public void Erase(string text)
{
    _textArray.Remove(text);
}
public void Erase(int textLevel)
{
    _textArray.RemoveAt(textLevel);
}
```

There is a method to display all the lines of text in order. When called, this displays the *current* lines of text in the array list:

```
public string ReadDocument()
{
    System.Text.StringBuilder sb = new
        System.Text.StringBuilder();
    foreach(string text in _textArray)
        sb.Append(text);
    return sb.ToString();
}
}
```

We need a way to introduce redo/undo functionality into our document object. In the solution we will see how the Command pattern accomplishes just that by storing commands as requests for a document.

Solution: Use a command as the request to store the text and allow the command to handle undo and redo requests of the document

To allow historical requests on our document and redo/undo functionality on those requests, we will use a Command class as a storage object for the request. Each command will house the text for the document and the methods to either undo or redo the text.

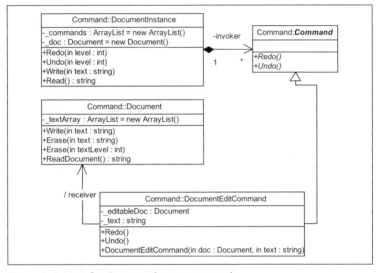

Figure 3-4. UML for Command pattern example

To give us the desired functionality we need to first create an abstract base class: Command. This class will serve as a contract for the inherited command classes. We have two abstract methods: Redo() and Undo(). These methods are to be implemented in the concrete classes and will contain references to methods on the Document object.

```
//base command
abstract class Command
{
    abstract public void Redo();
    abstract public void Undo();
}
```

Next we take a look at our concrete command class. Here we store the reference to the added text and a reference to our document. The text is part of the request and is how each request will modify the document:

```
//concrete implementation
class DocumentEditCommand : Command
{
    private Document _editableDoc;
    private string _text;

    public DocumentEditCommand(Document doc, string text)
    {
        _editableDoc = doc;
        _text = text;
        _editableDoc.Write(_text);
    }
```

Each of the parent class's abstract methods is overridden and implemented here, giving us references to the document's methods to add and subtract lines of text:

```
    override public void Redo()
    {
        _editableDoc.Write(_text);
    }
    override public void Undo()
    {
        _editableDoc.Erase(_text);
    }
}
```

Next we look at the `Invoker` object. This object serves as a repository for all request objects for this particular document.

```
//invoker
class DocumentInvoker
{
    private ArrayList _commands = new ArrayList();
```

We create and store a new document when the invoker instance is created. The invoker then can allow any command to access and modify the document's text.

```
    private Document _doc = new Document();
```

Which command is used on the document is based on the historical level, or the number of the request in the queue:

```
    public void Redo(int level)
    {
        Console.WriteLine("---- Redo {0} level ", level);
        ((Command)_commands[ level ]).Redo();
    }

    public void Undo(int level)
    {
        Console.WriteLine("---- Undo {0} level ", level);
        ((Command)_commands[ level ]).Undo();
    }
```

The document acts as the receiver of the action of the request and the invoker is the container for all the actions. Below, we see that the invoker class methods create and store commands, as well as apply them to the document:

```
    public void Write(string text)
    {
        DocumentEditCommand cmd = new
            DocumentEditCommand(_doc,text);
        _commands.Add(cmd);
```

```
    }

    public string Read()
    {
        return _doc.ReadDocument();
    }
}
```

Now we will look at how we can use the document's invoker and command relationship to perform undo and redo actions on the document. First, we need to add some text to the document:

```
DocumentInvoker instance = new DocumentInvoker ();
instance.Write("This is the original text.");
```

Here is the text so far:

```
This is the original text.--first write
```

Now we write another line into the `DocumentInvoker` instance:

```
instance.Write(" Here is some other text.");
This is the original text. Here is some other text.--second write
```

Next, to illustrate the usefulness of the command we perform an undo using the `DocumentInvoker`'s `Undo()` method, which will remove the last text from the document by using the `Command` class's `Undo()` method:

```
instance.Undo(1);
```

Here is the text now. Notice that the text has returned to its original state before the second write.

```
---- Undo 1 level
This is the original text.
```

After that we perform a redo with the same command. Notice this is possible because we store the text for the undo and redo within the command inside the invoker class.

```
instance.Redo(1);
```

Here is the text now. The text has been rewritten with the new text at the end.

```
---- Redo 1 level
This is the original text. Here is some other text.
```

We go on to perform undo and redo functions in a variety of operational orders to illustrate the flexible nature of the Command pattern strategy:

```
instance.Write(" And a little more text.");
instance.Undo(2);
instance.Redo(2);
instance.Undo(1);
```

And can see the results of our actions in the console window:

```
This is the original text. Here is some other text. And a little
more text.
---- Undo 2 level
This is the original text. Here is some other text.
---- Redo 2 level
This is the original text. Here is some other text. And a little
more text.
---- Undo 1 level
This is the original text. And a little more text.
```

Comparison to Similar Patterns

Commands and Mementos have some similarity due to the fact they both work with an object's internal properties. The Command pattern keeps a record of changes to an object's state and applies those changes in an ad-hoc fashion. A Memento pattern also records changes to an object's state, and can restore that state at any time. The Chain of Responsibility pattern seems to handle processing in a similar manner to the Command, except it hands off processing to another process linearly. An Interpreter pattern works in the example above because we are using language elements to determine which changes to apply at a given time.

What We Have Learned

Commands are useful tools when dealing with behaviors in objects. By making the request to an object a command object and storing the command in an invoker object, we can modify and keep historical records of different actions performed on an object. Virtually any action could be stored as a command and used to process requests in a variety of operational orders on a receiving object.

Related Patterns

- Chain of Responsibility pattern
- Composite pattern
- Interpreter pattern
- Memento pattern
- Template pattern

Behavioral Patterns

Interpreter Pattern

What Is an Interpreter Pattern?

The *Interpreter* pattern interprets language elements into code solutions. Interpreters can be used for various purposes including handling regular expressions or reading flat files to interpret *metadata* into code. Generally, if you have some language or textual data that you need to deal with as a code process, you might use an interpreter to convert the data into a code-recognizable form.

The Interpreter pattern has two main components associated with it: the *Context* and the *Expression*. The context acts as a current data context, defining the language data as it is before the interpretation. The expression component contains the logic to convert a particular context into a code-readable form.

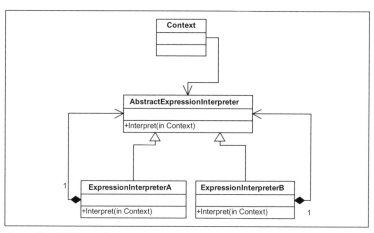

Figure 3-5. UML for Interpreter pattern

I use interpreters mostly for grabbing metadata from a *configuration file* or XML file and using that metadata to build code bases via reflection. I will show you in the examples two uses for interpreters that you may find interesting. One will deal with metadata conversion to code bases; the other follows the more traditional form of the pattern and converts dates based on the expression/context relationship.

Problem 1: The format of a date needs to be different depending on the particular type of date expression needed

Let's say for this first example that we need to have a date formatted in a particular way and this format could change depending on the date expression used. Right now we have an `if...then...else` code block that performs this action, but we need this code to be encapsulated in a class or method so it can be used against any context of date that we wish to use it for. In other words, we need to build a language expression engine around this code so that we can use objects instead of Boolean logic to evaluate which expression we need for which context:

```
if(IsWordDate)
    formattedDate = date.DayOfYear + "th day, " +
            date.DayOfWeek + ", " +
            ConvertMonth(date.Month) + " " +
            ConvertDay(date.Day)+", " +
            date.Year;
else if(IsCalendarDate)
    formattedDate = date.Month + "-" +
            date.Day+"-" +
            date.Year;
else if (IsGregorianDate)
    formattedDate = date.Month + "-" +
```

```
        date.Day+"-" +      date.Year + " " +
        date.Hour + ":" + date.Minute + ":" +
        date.Millisecond;
```

Solution 1: Use an interpreter and expression engine to manage the different date formats by expression type

A typical use of the Interpreter pattern is to allow different expressions to react to the context of language elements. Allowing expressions to be created as objects that can interpret the different context patterns of language elements allows the expression to be created in code from the language element.

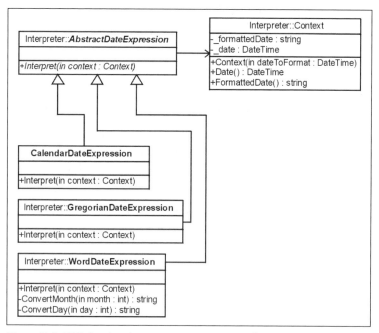

Figure 3-6. UML for date Interpreter pattern example

To accomplish the task in our problem above, we first need to turn our language context into an object. The context includes the actual language value and the interpreted value. For the example purposes this allows a date context to be altered by an expression type. We make our context into an object holding the date value and a placeholder for the formatted value from the expression.

```
class Context
{
    private string _formattedDate;
    private DateTime _date;
```

We hold our date value in an instance variable that is input in our constructor. We can get it back via a getter property method.

```
public Context(DateTime dateToFormat)
{
    _date = dateToFormat;
}
public DateTime Date
{
    get{return _date;}
}
```

We also have a property for accessing our formatted value. This will get set in our interpreter.

```
public string FormattedDate
{
    get{return _formattedDate;}
    set{_formattedDate = value;}
}
}
```

Next, we need to make our expression into an object. The expression is how the context is interpreted. We can have an expression for any type of interpretation we wish to have. For this example, we create a series of date expressions from an abstract parent class. Our abstract class holds a public abstract method that takes in our context class:

```
//interpreters
abstract class AbstractDateExpression
{
    public abstract void Interpret(Context context);
}
```

Each concrete expression has a different interpretation algorithm to alter the context:

```
class WordDateExpression : AbstractDateExpression
{
    public override void Interpret(Context context)
    {
        context.FormattedDate = date.DayOfYear + "th day, " +
            date.DayOfWeek + ", " +
            ConvertMonth(date.Month) + " " +
            ConvertDay(date.Day)+", " +
            date.Year;
    }
}

class CalendarDateExpression : AbstractDateExpression
{
    public override void Interpret(Context context)
    {
        context.FormattedDate = date.Month + "-" +
            date.Day+"-" +     date.Year;
    }
}

class GregorianDateExpression : AbstractDateExpression
{
    public override void Interpret(Context context)
    {
        context.FormattedDate = date.Month + "-" +
```

```
            date.Day+"-" +      date.Year + " " +
            date.Hour + ":" + date.Minute + ":" +
            date.Millisecond;
    }
}
```

As we pass the date context into each expression, that expression changes the value of the context to its particular interpretation of that context:

```
AbstractDateExpression exp = new WordDateExpression();
exp.Interpret(context);
```

Here we see the results for this interpretation:

```
Format for WordDateExpression:202th day, Friday, July
```

Our next interpretation of the context is for a calendar date:

```
exp = new CalendarDateExpression();
exp.Interpret(context);
```

And the results for our calendar conversion of the same date:

```
Format for CalendarDateExpression:7-21-2006
```

This is the interpretation of the Gregorian date format:

```
exp = new GregorianDateExpression();
exp.Interpret(context);
```

And the results for the Gregorian conversion of the date:

```
Format for GregorianDateExpression:7-21-2006 15:47:95
```

Behavioral Patterns

Problem 2: We need to create classes from metadata from remote packages or assemblies and load them using a common interpreter

For our next real-world problem we have a need to use metadata to determine class types at run time and load those class types instead of compiled references to the class types. Our metadata comes from an XML or config file and tells us the package and class name to load. We are doing this to allow an outside source to provide us the class types and use a common interpreter to load all these types. We need to do this to allow multiple assemblies or packages that have no compiled references to each other to interact in a common code base. Below we see the classes as they are constructed now. Currently these classes reside in the current code base, but for purposes of extensibility and a mandated change of scope we have to move them to a separate assembly or package.

```
class LoadOne{}
class LoadTwo{}

LoadOne one = new LoadOne();
LoadTwo two = new LoadTwo();
```

Here we have the metadata we are going to use to load the classes from the remote package or assembly from the XML file. Notice that we identify the name and the path inside the assembly to the class, along with the class name. (For this example we have not set the metadata to include the assembly or package path, but this is easy to implement.)

```
<?xml version="1.0" encoding="utf-8" ?>
<interpreter>
    <classes>
        <class name="LoadOne" path="Examples.Interpreter.LoadOne" />
```

```
        <class name="LoadTwo" path="Examples.Interpreter.LoadTwo" />
    </classes>
</interpreter>
```

Solution 2: Allow an interpreter to create the classes from metadata using reflection to recurse into the remote assemblies or packages

We will use our compiler and code language's reflection API extensively to be able to recurse into the code identified in our metadata for this solution. We will use reflection in an interpreter to read and interpret the assembly or package in which the class to load exists.

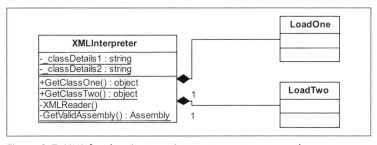

Figure 3-7. UML for class instance Interpreter pattern example

This type of interpreter seems very different from the pattern implementation in the previous solution. It is, however, one use of an Interpreter pattern that I think is very relevant. We are interpreting the language elements in the XML file to render code. So we are not straying too far from the letter of what interpreters do.

Below we see our interpreter class:

```
class XMLInterpreter
{
```

Since we are reading from an XML file, we have an internal method that performs this read. Our XML reader could take any form, but for this example we simply import the XML file into a .NET DataSet, which does most of the work for us:

```
private static void XMLReader()
{
```

We need the path to the metadata file to interpret. For this example we are looking in the same directory as our executable:

```
string path = Path.GetDirectoryName(
    GetValidAssembly().CodeBase.Replace(@"file:///","")) +
    Path.DirectorySeparatorChar + "Interpreter.xml";
```

We read our XML metadata into a dataset:

```
DataSet _dsDataSet = new DataSet();
DataView _dvDataView = null;
try
{

    _dsDataSet.ReadXml(path);
    _dvDataView = _dsDataSet.Tables[0].DefaultView;
    _dvDataView.AllowEdit = true;
    _dvDataView.AllowDelete = true;
    _dvDataView.AllowNew = true;

}
catch(Exception)
{

}
```

Next, we filter out the `DataSet` to a `DataTable` so we can see our XML file as data within the table:

```
DataTable table = _dvDataView.DataViewManager
                .DataSet.Tables["class"];
```

And last we filter and retrieve our XML metadata:

```
table.DefaultView.RowFilter="name='LoadOne'";
DataRowView row = table.DefaultView[0];
_classDetails1 = Convert.ToString(row["path"]);

table.DefaultView.RowFilter="name='LoadTwo'";
row = table.DefaultView[0];
_classDetails2 = Convert.ToString(row["path"]);
    }
}
```

As we said above, the way we get our metadata is not a factor; we could use a database or read XML from a file. The example above is just a sample of what we might do.

In our interpreter class we also have two methods to return the remote class types using the reflective method `Activator.CreateInstance`. Using this method we can load types we derive from the language elements we read from the config file. Our two methods return primitive object types.

```
public static object GetClassOne()
{
    if(_classDetails1 == null || _classDetails1 == string.Empty)
        XMLReader();
    return Activator.CreateInstance
            (Type.GetType(_classDetails1));
}
public static object GetClassTwo()
{
    if(_classDetails1 == null || _classDetails1 == string.Empty)
```

```
        XMLReader();
    return Activator.CreateInstance
        (Type.GetType(_classDetails2));
 }
```

> **Note:**   In the methods above we could define an
> expected return type, which would change this
> interpreter into a class factory.

If we wanted to we could provide more data, such as the path of the assembly or package for accessing remote code bases. For this example, we perform a simpler reflective recursion into the assembly structure by looking in the current directory for the assembly or for a registered assembly:

```
object class1 = XMLInterpreter.GetClassOne();
object class2 = XMLInterpreter.GetClassTwo();
```

We load our classes using our reflective class loader and we can then use them as needed:

```
ClassType for class 1:LoadOne
ClassType for class 2:LoadTwo
```

Comparison to Similar Patterns

The Factory pattern and the Interpreter pattern seem to have various similarities, especially when you factor in reflection. A Factory that creates classes based on reflection basically is an Interpreter if it uses metadata to define the class structure and path of the object it instantiates. Flyweights and other factory-driven patterns might also use this pattern to load data as needed for shared class types.

What We Have Learned

Interpreters allow us to take pieces of language from sources outside the code and implement them as code results. Basically, anytime you need any kind of conversion from textual contexts to code contexts, Interpreters are useful.

Related Patterns

■ Command pattern
■ Factory pattern
■ Flyweight pattern

Iterator Pattern

What Is an Iterator Pattern?

Iterators allow sequential access of elements in a collection of objects without exposing its underlying code. What does this mean? If you have a list object and you wish to move through each element in the list sequentially and maintain your current place in the list, an iterator seems appropriate. Iterator patterns have been around a long time. In early Visual Basic, iterators came in the form of record sets with methods to move through the record set and keep the current row as the placeholder. Earlier than that, iterators in different forms existed in other languages. Almost anyone familiar with coding languages has used an iterator in some form.

The Iterator pattern has two classes that are associated with it: the *Aggregate* and the *Iterator*. The aggregate is a collection or aggregate object of some type whose elements we wish to iterate through. We use the iterator as a tool to move through the aggregate elements and keep track of the progress.

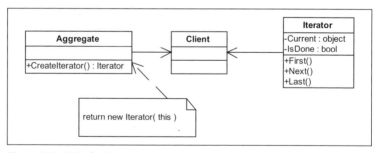

Figure 3-8. UML for Iterator pattern

Problem: A list object needs a way to move through each element in the list in consecutive order, retaining the position of the current record

For our example problem, we have a list adapter class that encapsulates and hides the functionality of an `ArrayList`. We need a way to determine which row we are on and keep a placeholder for that row, so that when we next access the list we can get the next object. In our current object we have standard methods for the list object represented in the adapter:

```
class List
{
```

A private array list object is adapted to hold our data:

```
    private ArrayList _listItems = new ArrayList();
```

We have ways to check the number of records in our underlying collection:

```
    public int Count
    {
        get{ return _listItems.Count; }
    }
```

We can add and remove items with adapted methods for the underlying collection:

```
    public void Append(object item)
    {
        _listItems.Add(item);
    }

    public void Remove(object item)
    {
        _listItems.Remove(item);
    }
```

Behavioral Patterns

```
public void RemoveAt(int index)
{
    _listItems.RemoveAt(index);
}
```

We can also get an item by supplying an index to a certain record:

```
public object this[ int index ]
{
    get{ return _listItems[ index ]; }
    set{ _listItems[index] = value; }
}

}
```

Our problem is to build a device that moves through our list object and records the current place in that object each time we access a record. We will need methods to move forward and back inside the list, and all this functionality should be included inside the list object.

Solution: Create a list iterator that keeps the current record position and has methods to read and move to the next record or to any record in the list

The iterator will give us a method to move concurrently through the list object's elements while keeping track between calls to the list of the location of the current record. We will need to derive the iterator from the List class to ensure that our iterator object contains a reference to the list.

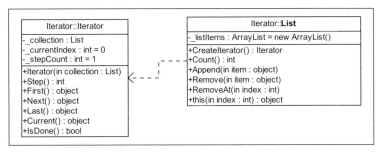

Figure 3-9. UML for Iterator pattern example

Our `List` class is already a good placeholder for the method to derive the iterator. We need to add a method to create a new iterator that holds the current list as a reference:

```
class List
{

    ....

    public Iterator CreateIterator()
    {
        return new Iterator(this);
    }
}
```

Next we need to create the actual iterator class. We will need private variables for the list object, the current record index, and the number of records to skip between each read or step count:

```
//iterator
class Iterator
{
    private List _collection;
    private int _currentIndex = 0;
    private int _stepCount = 1;
```

Behavioral Patterns

We need to define the iterator object's constructor as receiving the `List` class as its input parameter. This is done to hold the reference to the list object from the point of creation of the iterator.

```
public Iterator(List collection)
{
    this._collection = collection;
}
```

Then we need an accessor for the step count. This will allow us to change the number of records between each read to the list.

```
public int Step
{
    get{ return _stepCount; }
    set{ _stepCount = value; }
}
```

We need methods to iterate between records that will increment the current index or placeholder within the list by the step count and return the next object in the list. We have three methods defined for this example. There is a method to get the first record in the list, a method to get the last record, and a method to increment the list index by the step count and return the next record.

```
public object First()
{
    _currentIndex = 0;
    return _collection[ _currentIndex ];
}

public object Next()
{
    _currentIndex += _stepCount;
    if(!IsDone())
```

```
            return _collection[ _currentIndex ];
        else
            return null;
}

public object Last()
{
    _currentIndex = _collection.Count - 1;
    return _collection[ _currentIndex ];
}
```

We also have a method to return the current object in the list to the index of the iterator:

```
public object Current()
{
    return _collection[ _currentIndex ];
}
```

And last we need a method to indicate if we are at the end of the list:

```
public bool IsDone()
{
    return _currentIndex >= _collection.Count ? true : false ;
}
```

To begin the test of our iterator, we call the Create-Iterator() method to create our Iterator class and set the step to a value to skip to every third record:

```
Iterator skipIterator = list.CreateIterator();
skipIterator.Step = 3;
```

To test how our iterator gets each element in the list, we construct a for...loop. We use the First() method to return the first record in a for...loop. We use the IsDone() method to check for the last row and the Next() method to return the next record in the list.

```
for(object item = skipIterator.First();
    !skipIterator.IsDone(); item = skipIterator.Next())
```

Then we run the iterator and see we have returned every third record:

```
Skip to every third step
object 0
object 3
object 6
```

Next, we set the step to get every other record in the list from the iterator:

```
skipIterator.Step = 2;
Skip every other step
object 0
object 2
object 4
object 6
object 8
```

Last, we test the iterator to return every record. We set the step to 1 to indicate we get every record in the list from the first to the last:

```
skipIterator.Step = 1;
Skip no steps
object 0
object 1
object 2
object 3
object 4
object 5
object 6
object 7
object 8
```

Comparison to Similar Patterns

The Iterator pattern can be compared to the Memento pattern in the way it encapsulates the functionality of the aggregate and moves this logic to another class object, maintaining the state of the aggregate inside the iterator. This works much like the Memento pattern, which keeps state in the memento object until it is needed again. However, in the Memento the state is preserved as it was when removed from the originator. In the Iterator the state is changed directly inside the iterator. The iterator acts as an intermediary between the aggregate and itself, in effect acting as a mediator for itself, similar to the Mediator pattern.

What We Have Learned

The Iterator pattern can be a handy way to loop through a list and maintain the list's state and position. If it is important to keep your position in the list or to get only a smaller search of a group of records, the Iterator might be a useful pattern to implement. If a list needs to have every record processed in turn and the next cannot be processed before the first, then the Iterator can handle the placement of each object in the list and help the code only return the record needed in a sequential fashion.

Related Patterns

- Composite pattern
- Mediator pattern
- Memento pattern

Mediator Pattern

What Is a Mediator Pattern?

The *Mediator* pattern allows groups of objects to communicate in a disassociated manner and encapsulates this communication while keeping the objects loosely coupled. If you have a group of objects that need to communicate in some way, but you don't wish to allow them direct access to one another, then using this pattern would be a way to encapsulate this communication in a single object. The pattern allows objects to communicate on a one-to-one basis and acts as a proxy between objects to facilitate this communication.

The Mediator pattern has two main classes associated with it: the *Mediator* and the *Colleague*. The mediator acts as a go-between to the colleagues and controls which two colleagues communicate. The concrete mediator and concrete colleague act as implementation classes with their abstract bases defining the interaction.

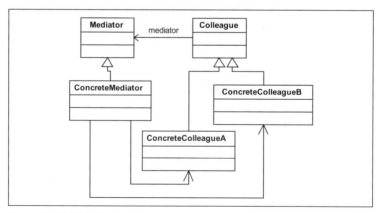

Figure 3-10. UML for Mediator pattern

Many times you find yourself needing to have several objects of similar types communicate in some way with each other. But often this communication can become too entangled and the methods of communication too deeply coupled or too rigid to make changes easily. Using a mediator you can register groups of objects, thus encapsulating the means of communication inside the mediator. After registering each class you then can specify a message in one object and have that message sent to another registered object without either object having a compiled reference to the other. This is especially useful since multiple class instances can be registered inside the mediator at run time and will be able to communicate between each other without having to know about each other directly.

Problem: Message windows reference each other directly, and if new windows are added the code cannot easily manage each window's reference to the other

We start this problem with two message windows that both have some methods for sending and receiving messages. Right now these message windows can communicate directly. But if we needed to add several instances of these windows and control their communication, the code to do this would quickly become very complex.

```
MessageThread imWindow = new IMWindow("Jazzy Jeff");
MessageThread chatWindow = new ChatWindow("Sir Chats-A-Lot");

imWindow.Receive(chatWindow.Name, "Hey Jazzy!");
chatWindow.Receive(imWindow.Name, "Hey Sir Chats-A-Lot!");
```

We need a way to control how the messages get sent between the message windows. The method we use should allow us to add new window instances with a common base type. Each window should not have a direct reference to any other, and messages should be handed between windows by a third party. Also, since the message windows exist on client machines we need a way to allow remote communication between the different clients via a server object and allow that server object to manage each connection. Let's take a look at how the Mediator pattern helps us do this.

Solution: Use a mediator to control messages between each window

The first step to using the Mediator pattern to solve our problem is to build our mediator to control the communication between the message window instances. The mediator we will use has two parts: an *abstract mediator* and a *concrete mediator*. Why do we need the two parts? Suppose you wanted to define multiple mediator class types. Making an abstract as a contract and allowing concrete instances is more flexible than defining one type. However, defining an abstract is not necessary, except for the fact that to communicate remotely across multiple threads as message windows do from client to client, they need to reference an interface to the server application.

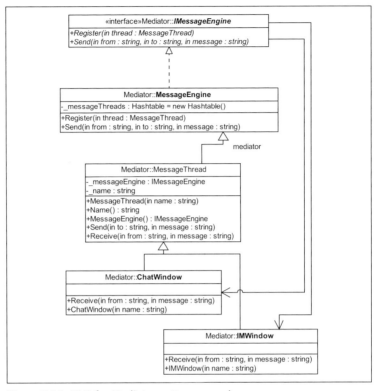

Figure 3-11. UML for Mediator pattern example

The abstract mediator in this example is an interface. The server application manages the multiple connections of the client message windows and allows one message window instance to send and receive messages to another instance registered with the server. The abstract mediator interface allows remote access from each client window into the server that controls which messages get sent between the registered clients. We use the `IMessageEngine` interface in this example to accommodate this:

```
interface IMessageEngine
{
```

```
    void Register(MessageThread thread);
    void Send(string from, string to, string message);
}
```

> **Note:** We are not taking into account TCP/IP
> handlers or client connection handling and managing
> connections remotely for this example. For a realistic
> client-server interface, obviously more work is involved,
> but this is beyond the scope of this example.

Next we create our concrete mediator class. This is the class
that would reside on the server and allow different window
client objects to register themselves and send communication messages to the server mediator, which in turn would
redirect these messages to the proper client window.

```
class MessageEngine : IMessageEngine
{
```

Notice we have a collection of message window objects and
a method to register new ones into the collection. Upon
registration of the message window, the server mediator
object adds a reference to itself to the `MessageThread`
class instance to provide access back to the server.

```
    private Hashtable _messageThreads = new Hashtable();
    public void Register(MessageThread thread)
    {
        if(!_messageThreads.ContainsKey(thread.Name))
            _messageThreads.Add(thread.Name,thread);

        thread.MessageEngine = this;
    }
```

We also have a method to send messages to the server. The method finds the desired window to send the message to and sends it to the `Receive()` method of that window. This differs from the current solution in that each window is disconnected from references to other windows. The server interface manages each remote window from different clients.

```
public void Send(string from, string to, string message)
{
    MessageThread thread = (MessageThread)_messageThreads[ to ];
    if(thread != null)
        thread.Receive(from, message);
}
}
```

Next, to finish the mediator implementation we modify our `MessageThread` class, adding an accessor to the `IMessageEngine` interface:

```
abstract class MessageThread
{
    private IMessageEngine _messageEngine;
    .....

    public IMessageEngine MessageEngine
    {
        set{ _messageEngine = value; }
        get{ return _messageEngine; }
    }
```

We also add a reference to the `Send()` method on the server mediator object. This allows our client message windows to send each message back to the server and have the mediator object decide and send the message to the proper receiver message window.

```
public void Send(string to, string message)
{
    _messageEngine.Send(_name, to, message);
}
}
```

When we look at the example at run time, we can see how the code flows between the client windows. If we send a message to another client through our server mediator, it gets redirected to the proper receiver client via its `Receive()` method:

```
//Create the message engine which is the mediator
IMessageEngine engine = new MessageEngine();

//instantiate two chat instance message windows
MessageThread imWindow = new IMWindow("Jazzy Jeff");
MessageThread chatWindow = new ChatWindow("Sir Chats-A-Lot");

//Register each chat instance window with the mediator
engine.Register(imWindow);
engine.Register(chatWindow);

//Jazzy Jeff sends a message to Sir Chats-A-Lot
imWindow.Send("Sir Chats-A-Lot","Hey Sir Chats-A-Lot!");

Output: -----------
ChatWindow Received: Jazzy Jeff to Sir Chats-A-Lot:
'Hey Sir Chats-A-Lot!'

// Sir Chats-A-Lot sends a message back to Jazzy Jeff
chatWindow.Send("Jazzy Jeff","Hey Jazzy!");

Output: -----------
IMWindow Received: Sir Chats-A-Lot to Jazzy Jeff: 'Hey Jazzy!'
```

We could now add any number of client message windows without modifying our code. Since we allow the server to decide which windows communicate and handle the mapping to that communication, direct window references are no longer necessary.

Comparison to Similar Patterns

A Mediator pattern at first blush seems similar to an Observer pattern. The main difference is how it is implemented. The Mediator takes a group of classes and allows these classes to communicate between one another without having access to each other. This is done in a one-to-one fashion. An Observer pattern keeps a group of classes that is linked to it updated in a one-to-many fashion. So the Mediator allows decoupled communication between a pair of classes, and an Observer allows communication between one class and many other classes linked to it.

What We Have Learned

Mediators are useful when we need to control references between objects for purposes of sending or receiving data. If we wish to expand a relatively static code model into a more object-handled pattern, we can use mediators to control the program flow of how these independent objects communicate.

Related Patterns

- Iterator pattern
- Memento pattern
- Observer pattern
- Template pattern

Behavioral Patterns

Memento Pattern

What Is a Memento Pattern?

The *Memento* pattern is a way to capture an object's internal state without violating encapsulation of the object, and preserve that state for some purpose. That means if we have some values for an object we wish to preserve outside the object and these values do not necessarily have external access from that object and we do not wish to provide external access to these values because it would violate the encapsulation rules of the object, we can use a Memento pattern to hold these data points or *states*. State management in this fashion gives us a snapshot of data for an object. We could then use the preserved values to restore the object's state at any time.

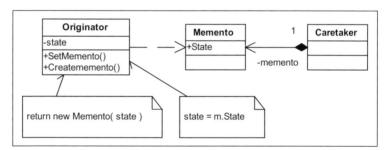

Figure 3-12. UML for Memento pattern

Memento patterns have three main objects associated to perform the work of the pattern: the *Originator,* the *Care-Taker,* and the *Memento*. The originator is the class whose internal state we wish to capture. The memento class is the class in which we store the originator's state. The caretaker class stores the memento until it is needed to restore that state to the originator.

Problem: A class needs to have its internal state captured and then restored without violating the class's encapsulation

Our example illustrates a common problem with encapsulation in classes. We have a class that contains some data. This data is the state of the object for a particular instance in time. If we should wish to preserve that state for some reason (perhaps for a refresh back to the original), the only way to accurately capture the entire state would be to allow access to each data point on the object. This would violate the encapsulation of the object, exposing variables that are set internally to the class. But if we did not wish to provide direct access to values set internally, we could not capture the current state.

For our example, we have the object `Product` that has some externally accessible variables and one that is internally set: `State`. An enumeration is used to indicate the different types of state within the object:

```
enum State{NEW,LOADED,CHANGED};

//Originator
class Product
{
    private string _name;
    private string _description;
    private double _cost;
    private State _state = State.NEW;
```

The class's constructor takes in the initial values and sets the internal state variable to LOADED. This marks the class as initialized and loaded with data.

```
public Product(string name, string description, double cost)
{
    _name = name;
    _description = description;
    _cost = cost;
    _state = State.LOADED;
}
```

Our values have getter/setter properties, while our internal enum for indicating state has no outside access at this time:

```
public string Name
{
    get{return _name;}
    set{_name = value;_state = State.CHANGED;}
}
public string Description
{
    get{return _description;}
    set{_description = value;_state = State.CHANGED;}
}
public double Cost
{
    get{return _cost;}
    set{_cost = value;_state = State.CHANGED;}
}
public State State
{
    get{return _state;}
}
}
```

The obvious problem is that if we wanted to restore the original complete state of the object we could not do this without allowing external access to the state variable. We need a way to preserve the complete state without allowing access to the state variable in order to keep from violating the encapsulation rules of the class.

Solution: Use a memento and a caretaker to capture and store the object's state

From the problem above we see that we have to maintain the encapsulation of the `Product` object and still capture and restore the full state of the object. To accomplish this we will use the Memento pattern to establish a class object that is internal to `Product` to capture and store its state.

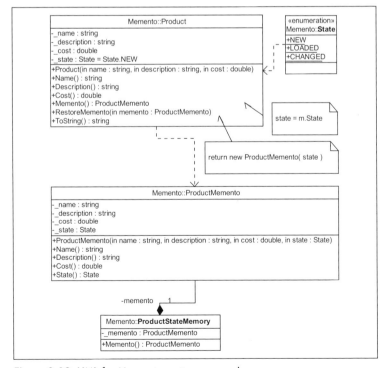

Figure 3-13. UML for Memento pattern example

The first step is to create our memento class. The memento class contains all the variables of `Product` that will be needed to restore the object's state at a later time. These variables are fed into the input parameters of the class's constructor:

```
//Memento
class ProductMemento
{
    .....
    public ProductMemento(string name, string description,
                        double cost, State state)
    {
        this._name = name;
        this._description = description;
        this._cost = cost;
        this._state = state;
    }
```

Since we only wish to modify the memento at creation to maintain the proper state, each variable on the memento is read only:

```
public string Name
{
    get{return _name;}
}
public string Description
{
    get{return _description;}
}
public double Cost
{
    get{return _cost;}
}
public State State
{
```

```
        get{return _state;}
    }
}
```

Next, we need a place to store the memento object until it is needed again by the `Product` class. The Memento pattern defines just such an object: the caretaker. The caretaker object houses our memento until such time as our instance of the `Product` needs to have its state restored:

```
//Caretaker
class ProductStateMemory
{
    // Fields
    private ProductMemento _memento;

    // Properties
    public ProductMemento Memento
    {
        set{ _memento = value; }
        get{ return _memento; }
    }
}
```

The last step to implement the Memento pattern is to place a method to create the memento inside the `Product` object. This gives the memento object internal access to all the variables of `Product`. This `ProductMemento` class will be created internally to the `Product` object. Because it is internal, it is allowed access to all the state variables encapsulated inside the object. Then, at a later time, we can return the object to the class and let the `Product` class use the `ProductMemento` to restore its complete internal state.

We need two methods to accomplish this. The first will create the `ProductMemento` object's internal variables:

```
//Originator with memento methods
class Product
{
    ......
    public ProductMemento Memento
    {
        get{return new ProductMemento(_name, _description,
                                      _cost, _state);}
    }
```

The second will restore the `Product` object's internal state by passing it back the `ProductMemento` class:

```
    public void RestoreMemento(ProductMemento memento)
    {
        this._name = memento.Name;
        this._description = memento.Description;
        this._cost = memento.Cost;
        this._state = memento.State;
    }
}
```

Now let's take a look at how the Memento pattern performs during run time. First, we create our `Product` object, initializing the internal variables with input parameters in the constructor. This sets the internal `State` variable from `NEW` to `LOADED`:

```
Product product = new Product("Product A","The first Product
                              in inventory",50.00);
```

And we can see the variables indeed have the expected values:

```
Name:Product A
Description:The first Product in inventory
Cost:50
State:LOADED
```

Next, we call the method on `Product` to create our memento. We store this inside our caretaker object `ProductStateMemory` for later use:

```
ProductStateMemory memory = new ProductStateMemory();
memory.Memento = product.Memento;
```

Now we can change our `Product` object's variables as we wish:

```
product.Name = "Product A(2)";
product.Description = "We have a change";
product.Cost = 60.00;
```

And see these changes are indeed reflected in the class:

```
Change the object:
Name:Product A(2)
Description:We have a change
Cost:60
State:CHANGED
```

To restore the state of the `Product` object, we simply pass the memento from our caretaker object back into the `Product` object via the `RestoreMemento()` method:

```
product.RestoreMemento(memory.Memento);
```

A look at the class values shows us that our original state for the `Product` object has been restored by the memento:

```
Restore state via the memento....
Name:Product A
Description:The first Product in inventory
Cost:50
State:LOADED
```

Behavioral Patterns

Comparison to Similar Patterns

The Memento pattern is similar to the Command pattern in that we are storing separately from the object a state or change to its internal values. It is similar to the Observer pattern in that both patterns use attributes of the target object passed to initialize or change values inside the pattern subject. It can be compared in somewhat the same manner to the Mediator, in that it holds and maintains control of data for another object.

What We Have Learned

Memento patterns allow us to beat the rules of encapsulation when dealing with classes with internal states that are inaccessible without violating the encapsulation of a class. We can use a memento to capture and store a class's state, and then restore that state at any time.

Related Patterns

- Command pattern
- Iterator pattern
- Mediator pattern
- Observer pattern
- State pattern

Observer Pattern

What Is an Observer Pattern?

The *Observer* pattern facilitates communication between a parent class and any dependent child classes, allowing changes to the state of the parent class to be sent to the dependent child classes. We can use this pattern to allow the state changes in a class to be sent to all its dependent classes. The class relationship is one-to-many between the class and all its dependents.

The pattern generally consists of two base classes. The first is called the *Subject* class, and this class acts as the notification engine. The *Observer* classes act as receivers of the subject notifications. From these two base class types the concrete implementations for each type are derived: *concrete subject* and *concrete observer*.

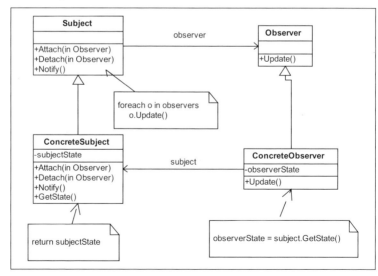

Figure 3-14. UML for Observer pattern

Observers generally monitor the state of a class they are linked to and get information from that class when changes occur that they are concerned about. If we had a class that linked into many classes, and those classes wished to know about changes within it, we might use this pattern. The pattern allows code to handle the notifications automatically through the structure of the objects, instead of letting Boolean logic decide. It also offers a cleaner and more intuitive way to allow communication between a single object supplying notifications and its dependent objects.

Problem: We have several child forms of an MDI form that we need to inform of changes that occur in the MDI form, and we have no way to do this automatically

For our example problem, we need to notify a series of child classes when an MDI (multiple document interface) form changes its title.

We start out with a `Form` class and `MdiForm` class but have no way to inform each individual `Form` class that has the `MdiForm` as its parent of changes within the parent.

```
class Form
{
    private string _name;
    private string _title;
    public Form(string name)
    {
        _name = name;
    }
    public string Name
    {
        get{return _name;}
    }
```

```
public string Title
{
    get{return _title;}
    set{_title = value;}
}
}
```

The `MdiForm` inherits from the `Form` class. Its children are all simple `Form` classes:

```
class MdiForm : Form
{
    private ArrayList _forms = new ArrayList();
    .....
}
```

Our problem is that we don't have a good way to inform the children of the `MdiForm` class of any changes in that class. We want our child forms to be notified each time the `MdiForm`'s title is changed, and reflect those changes in their titles.

Let's see how the Observer pattern can help us with this problem.

Solution: Use the Observer pattern to provide notifications to the child forms when the MDI form state is changed

For our solution to the problem we will use the Observer pattern to provide notifications to the MDI form's children without having to write code each time a change occurs. Instead, the `MdiForm` will notify all its children of its changes as they occur.

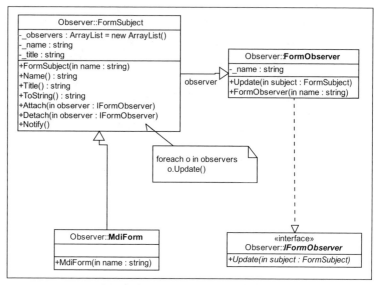

Figure 3-15. UML for Observer pattern example

We first need to change the classes to match the Observer pattern elements. Below we see we have refactored MdiForm into a class called FormSubject. This class is the subject class that controls the notifications of its observers. We will inherit the concrete MdiForm class from this class. Notice that we have an ArrayList to hold the observers, much as we had in the original MdiForm class:

```
abstract class FormSubject //refactored from Form
{
    private ArrayList _observers = new ArrayList();
    private string _name;
    private string _title;

    public FormSubject(string name)
    {
        _name = name;
    }
```

```
public string Name
{
    get{return _name;}
}
```

Notice that the Notify() method is called when the Title accessor is changed. This allows all attached observer objects to be notified of the change:

```
public string Title
{
    get{return _title;}
    set
    {
        _title = value;
        Notify();
    }
}
```

There are also methods to attach and remove the observer classes to and from the subject, allowing the subject to control the one-to-many relationship using the IFormObserver interface as a conduit to each observer:

```
public void Attach(IFormObserver observer)
{
    _observers.Add(observer);
}

public void Detach(IFormObserver observer)
{
    _observers.Remove(observer);
}
```

The Notify() method loops through each observer interface stored in the subject class and calls the Update() method on each. This will be how we notify each observer of changes to the subject class.

```
public void Notify()
{
    foreach(IFormObserver o in _observers)
        o.Update(this);
}
}
```

Now the `MdiForm` will inherit from the `FormSubject` class. This gives the control of notification to the `MdiForm` class.

```
//Concrete Subject
class MdiForm : FormSubject
{
    public MdiForm(string name) : base(name){}
}
```

We use the interface `IFormObserver` as the reference to the concrete observer. This actually is an alternative to the pattern's abstract observer class, and works the same way. Each observer interface accepts a reference to the subject in the `Update()` method to gain access to the subject's properties:

```
//Observer
interface IFormObserver
{
    void Update(FormSubject subject);
}
```

We implement the interface on each `FormObserver` object that we refactored from our `Form` class:

```
// "ConcreteObserver"
class FormObserver : IFormObserver
{
    private string _name;

    public FormObserver(string name)
    {
```

```
    _name = name;
  }
```

The `Update()` method from the interface is implemented on the `FormObserver` class, which utilizes the passed `FormSubject` instance to retrieve the state that we wish to notify the observer of:

```
public void Update(FormSubject subject)
{
    Console.WriteLine("Form Observer {0}'s new Title is '{1}'",
        _name, subject.Title);
}

}
```

When we examine the run-time behavior of the newly refactored classes we see that when our subject class `MdiForm` receives a change to its title, the `Notify()` method will send the change to each class that is attached to it. To demonstrate, we first create our `FormObserver` class instances, then our `FormSubject` instance as `MdiForm`:

```
IFormObserver formOb1 = new FormObserver("1");
IFormObserver formOb2 = new FormObserver("2");
IFormObserver formOb3 = new FormObserver("3");
IFormObserver formOb4 = new FormObserver("4");

FormSubject mdiForm = new MdiForm("MAIN MDI Form");
```

Next, we attach each observer class to the subject class. This allows the subject class to have a registry of attached objects to notify.

```
mdiForm.Attach(formOb1);
mdiForm.Attach(formOb2);
mdiForm.Attach(formOb3);
mdiForm.Attach(formOb4);
```

When we change the `Title` accessor for the MDI form, we can see that each observer child form receives that change when we make a change to the parent `MdiForm`'s `Title` property:

```
mdiForm.Title = "MDI Form Title Change #1";
Form Observer 1's new Title is 'MDI Form Title Change #1'
Form Observer 2's new Title is 'MDI Form Title Change #1'
Form Observer 3's new Title is 'MDI Form Title Change #1'
Form Observer 4's new Title is 'MDI Form Title Change #1'

mdiForm.Title = "MDI Form Title Change #2";
Form Observer 1's new Title is 'MDI Form Title Change #2'
Form Observer 2's new Title is 'MDI Form Title Change #2'
Form Observer 3's new Title is 'MDI Form Title Change #2'
Form Observer 4's new Title is 'MDI Form Title Change #2'
```

Comparison to Similar Patterns

I would say the main difference between Observer and Mediator patterns is how the objects communicate. In the Observer pattern, one object communicates with many linked objects. In the Mediator, objects in a group communicate on a one-to-one basis between each other without referencing each other. Observer subjects and singletons both pass values from a single object to many other objects. Observers use the state of the subject object and gain that state as a linked object. Observers use the state like a Memento pattern, storing parts of the state of the subject.

What We Have Learned

Observers are interesting ways to allow a one-to-many relationship for passing and sharing state between a subject and a number of observer objects. It allows an automatic relationship to be established between a subject and its observers that allows controlled information to be exchanged at key moments between these objects.

Related Patterns

- Mediator pattern
- Memento pattern
- Singleton pattern
- State pattern
- Template pattern

State Pattern

What Is a State Pattern?

The *State* pattern is a way to allow an object to change its behavior and functionality depending on its internal values. That is, when a value or attribute of an object changes, so too will its state. The state object controls the changes it makes or can be controlled by the context object in some cases and, depending on rules set up for the context, identifies these changes by changing itself into another object (or value in the case of an enum as an object state).

The State pattern has two main components: the *State* object and the *Context* object. The state object can change depending on factors associated with the context and identifies changes in the context based on which object representation the state is in at a given time. The state object uses values from the context to determine how the state of the context will change. The context object holds the state and is referenced by the state. It allows the state to change itself according to rules and data from the context.

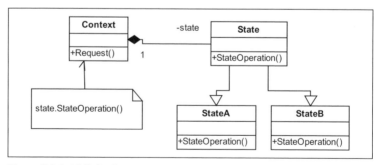

Figure 3-16. UML for State pattern

State management is very important to systems that either are maintained against multiple threads or requests, or span multiple systems. State in a class or object allows different processes to change an object and have other processes see the results of those changes. This is particularly useful to database or entity relational systems. Also, any systems that manage *unit of work* or transactional data and/or information usually use state management in some way.

Problem 1: We have no way to determine the state of an object without performing calculations outside an object

We need to define a way to determine what kind of changes have occurred on the context object by checking a single attribute. In our current code we have a data object named `Product` on which we need to monitor state. This object is simple enough, but we can't make any kind of determination about the object's current state or if that state has changed in any way without making some calculations outside the object. We need a way to determine if we are low on product or have enough when changes are made to the object. Below is the stateless object before we begin to refactor:

```
class Product
{
```

First, we see private variables indicating the name of the product, the number of items in stock, and the number sold:

```
private string _name;
private int _numberInStock;
private int _itemsSold;
```

The constructor takes in the basic information for our Product class such as the name and number of items in stock:

```
public Product(string name, int numberInStock)
{
    _name = name;
    _numberInStock = numberInStock;
}
```

We have properties for the variables we input in the constructor:

```
public string Name
{
    get{return _name;}
    set{_name = value;}
}

public int NumberInStock
{
    get{return _numberInStock;}
}
```

The `Sell()` method takes in the number of items sold, decrements the number in stock, and increments the internal variable for items sold:

```
public override void Sell(int itemsSold)
{
    if(itemsSold > _numberInStock)
    {
        itemsSold = _numberInStock;
        _numberSold += itemsSold;
        _numberInStock -= itemsSold;
    }
    else
    {
        _itemsSold += itemsSold;
        _numberInStock -= itemsSold;
    }
}
```

We also have a method to add new items for restock:

```
public override void Restock(int itemsRestocked)
{
    _numberInStock += itemsRestocked;
}
}
```

Notice the methods `Sell()` and `Restock()`. We are going to need to modify these methods to allow a more stateful management of the variables they modify.

Behavioral Patterns

Solution 1: Use a state object that can change itself as the context object changes to determine the context state

Our solution for this example is to build objects with polymorphic properties to encapsulate rules around the Product class's values and the state of those values. These objects will be our state objects and will also deal with how the values interact and are managed.

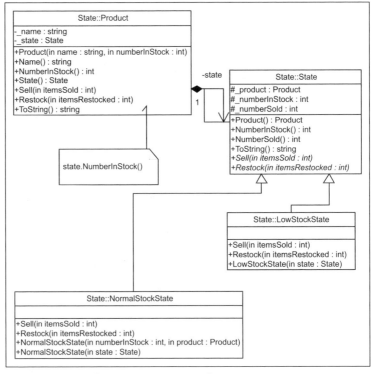

Figure 3-17. UML for State pattern example

Our first step is to create our base state class from which we will derive our concrete implementations for each state type. We do this by creating the abstract class State:

```
abstract class State
{
    protected Product _product;
    protected int _numberInStock;
    protected int _numberSold;
```

State holds a reference to the context object Product and holds current values for the number of products sold and in stock. We refactor State to hold these values so it can directly reference and manage each stateful value. This is not a mandatory way to manage these values since you always keep a reference to the context object, but it was the simpler implementation for this example.

```
    public Product Product
    {
        get{return _product;}
        set{_product = value;}
    }

    public int NumberInStock
    {
        get{return _numberInStock;}
    }

    public int NumberSold
    {
        get{return _numberSold;}
    }
```

We also define two abstract methods to be implemented on the concrete state classes. These methods provide the concrete state classes a way to define different implementations of functionality for each state. The methods for selling and restocking a product are going to be refactored from the product object to the state objects to have that functionality managed there. This allows the individual state to change this functionality as required for each state of the context object.

```
    abstract public void Sell(int itemsSold);
    abstract public void Restock(int itemsRestocked);
}
```

Next, we need to define our concrete state types. For this example we define two: LowStockState and NormalStockState. LowStockState is the state our Product object will reside in if the product stock reaches zero. Seeing this state on the object will tell us that we need to reorder and will not allow us to sell any more stock. NormalStockState is the state that is normal to the product. It tells us we have stock to sell.

The NormalStockState is our default state for the Product object. It contains two constructors: one to allow the product and number of stock to be passed in for initialization within the Product object, and one to allow control to be passed from the LowStockState state object.

```
class NormalStockState : State
{
    public NormalStockState(int numberInStock, Product product)
    {
        this._numberInStock = numberInStock;
        this._numberSold = 0;
        this._product = product;
    }
    public NormalStockState(State state)
    {
        this._numberInStock = state.NumberInStock;
```

```
    this._numberSold = state.NumberSold;
    this._product = state.Product;
}
```

The `Sell()` method of `NormalStockState` checks to
make sure we are not selling more than our current stock
and manages each sale by adding to the items sold variable
and subtracting from the items in stock. When the stock
dwindles to zero, it changes the state and hands the processing to the `LowStockState` object via the `Product`:

```
public override void Sell(int itemsSold)
{
    if(itemsSold >= _numberInStock)
    {
        _product.State = new LowStockState(this);
        _product.State.Sell(itemsSold);
    }
    else
    {
        _numberSold += itemsSold;
        _numberInStock -= itemsSold;
    }
}
```

Since restocking the product only changes the state if it is in
the `LowStockState` state, the `NormalStockState` state
object only adds to the product stock:

```
public override void Restock(int itemsRestocked)
{
    _numberInStock += itemsRestocked;
}
}
```

In our `LowStockState` constructor we pass in the values
from the preceding state to initialize the current state. Our
constructor only needs to be passed the previous state,
since it is never default:

```
class LowStockState : State
{

    public LowStockState(State state)
    {
        this._numberInStock = state.NumberInStock;
        this._numberSold = state.NumberSold;
        this._product = state.Product;
    }
}
```

If we look at the `LowStockState` representation of the `Sell()` method, we see we are checking to see if we have current quantities of stock, and if so we change our state to `NormalStockState`. We also pass back control to the `Product` object to allow it to determine the proper state to access to sell a product. If insufficient quantities of the stock are available, then this state manages how the stock is sold:

```
public override void Sell(int itemsSold)
{
    if(itemsSold >= _numberInStock)
    {
        itemsSold = _numberInStock;
        _numberSold += itemsSold;
        _numberInStock -= itemsSold;
    }
    else
    {
        _product.State = new NormalStockState(this);
        _product.State.Sell(itemsSold);
    }
}
```

The `Restock()` method works in a similar fashion, changing the product's state automatically to `Normal-StockState` when the new stock is added:

```
public override void Restock(int itemsRestocked)
{
```

```
    _numberInStock += itemsRestocked;
    _product.State = new NormalStockState(this);
  }
}
```

Now let's look at how the state changes both functionality and object type in the actual run-time workflow. We start off constructing a new `Product` object with 15 items:

```
Start with 'Product A' at quantity of 15—
```

Next we sell five items. This does not change our state, since we still have stock greater than zero:

```
Sell 5—
Name:Product A
State:NormalStockState, Number In Stock:10, Number Sold:5
```

Next we try to sell 11 items. Since we only have 10 items in stock, our state changes to `LowStockState` state and we only sell 10 items, which is the total of items in stock:

```
Sell 11—
Name:Product A
State:LowStockState, Number In Stock:0, Number Sold:15
```

Finally, we get in another 15 items and restock the product. The state is automatically changed back to `NormalStockState` state.

```
Restock 15—
Name:Product A
State:NormalStockState, Number In Stock:15, Number Sold:0
```

We can see each time we add or subtract items in the product that the state is changed and manages itself internally according to the rules set up for the `Product`. We can monitor the state simply by checking its implementation type on the `Product` object.

Behavioral Patterns

Problem 2: We need to prevent unsynchronized or dirty updates between factory class instantiation calls

For our second example I have chosen a scenario that I originally included in the factory section, but saw it seemed to pertain more directly to state management. It does not follow the letter of the pattern, but instead serves to illustrate another usage for state in regard to stateful object management within a synchronized repository.

We have discovered after using a factory that we need to have the states of our loaded factory objects maintained across multiple threads so that dirty updates can be handled and the states of loaded classes can be maintained. *Dirty updates* are when data from a data source has non-concurrent updates committed to its data. That is to say, if you pull some data from your data source, make a change to the data, and another process makes an update on the same data before you can make your update, then you make your update (in effect erasing the previous update), you have now committed a dirty update.

Solution 2: Make the factory a static interface, and maintain class states across multiple threads

To maintain state of our Suit classes between different process threads for purposes of determining whether a dirty update has occurred since data was last retrieved into the factory, we need to make the factory and its loaded class types accessible to multiple threads. To accomplish this, we make the factory a static one. We change the implementation of the dictionaries and the methods involved to make the factory accessible to any thread within the global process by marking them static:

```
private static Hashtable _registered = new Hashtable();
private static Hashtable _loaded = new Hashtable();
private static LOADSTATUS _loadStatus = LOADSTATUS.Ghost;

public static Suit CreateSuitWithState(SuitType suitType)
{
    if(_loaded[suitType] == null)
        Load();
    return (Suit)_loaded[suitType];
}
```

> **Note:** The static access modifier gives the method or attribute with this modifier global access; in other words, it gives access to any thread associated with the domain of the class. It also prevents instances of the class from having access to the method or attribute. This in effect provides any thread access to the method or attribute regardless of instance, and maintains the state of these across multiple threads involved in the global process.

Behavioral Patterns

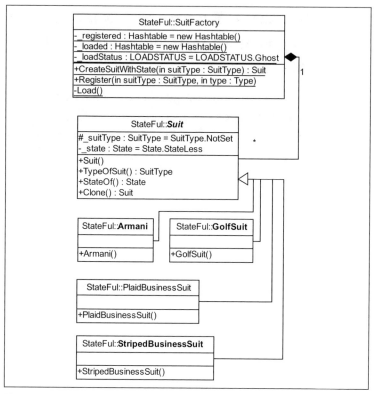

Figure 3-18. UML for State/Factory pattern example

We next need to modify our `Suit` class to include some parameters to indicate whether or not the particular instance has been modified. We use an enum class type `State` to indicate the class state inside the factory:

```
public abstract class Suit
{
    .......
    public enum State{StateLess, Loaded, Changed};
    public State StateOf
    {
        get{return _state;}
    }
```

Next, we need to modify the `Suit` class's access modifiers to change its state if modified. Since each `Suit` implementation class is stored within the static factory, when a thread changes some value of an attribute that we want to maintain for object state, we want to change the `State` enum value on the object to `Changed`. This maintains across multiple threads, so that even if a dirty update occurs, only the last change to the specific attribute gets saved. Marking the class as dirty is only the first step, however. The way to make sure a dirty update does not occur is to throw an exception or refuse the change when we change a value on an attribute for a class whose state is changed. That way, any attempts to change the attribute thereafter until the current update was committed and a fresh data source retrieve was done would fail. This would effectively keep dirty updates from occurring within the scope of the domain of the code base.

> **Warning:** Dirty updates to SQL data sources or any data source not running exclusively inside the global process (including data sources that are external or modifiable outside the domain) will still be possible even if you mark your classes with a dirty update status. This is due to the lack of synchronization between your code base and the data source. If multiple global processes are running for the same code base (as in the case of multiple servers in a web farm) and there is no way to access the data repository code across servers, the solution in this example alone would not prevent a dirty update between multiple repositories. To keep a dirty update from occurring in such a situation, your transactional code would have to include the actual outside data source and give final control to that data source for managing dirty updates.

Here we see the `Suit` class with its `TypeOfSuit` attribute set up for changing its state. Notice that if the `TypeOf-Suit` attribute is not set to the initialized form and the attribute value is changed, an exception is thrown. This is done to guarantee that a dirty update cannot be committed. Also, we change the state if the `Suit` class is not initialized.

```
public abstract class Suit
{
    public enum State{StateLess, Loaded, Changed};

    public SuitType TypeOfSuit
    {
        get{return _suitType;}
        set
        {
            if(_state == State.Changed)
                throw new Exception("Attribute 'TypeOfSuit' has
                    already been modified in another process and
                    cannot be modified again until the current
                    update has been committed.");
            if(value != _suitType)
                _state = State.Changed;

            _suitType = value;
        }
    }
    public State StateOf
    {
        get{return _state;}
    }
}
```

We determine our `SuitType` enum inside the constructor of the suit class implementation:

```
public class GolfSuit : Suit
{
    public GolfSuit(){ _suitType = SuitType.GolfSuit;}
}
```

Our factory object will be the managing code repository for all `Suit` classes. We have two collections to manage the objects. One will house the allowed types as registered entities, and the other will house all the loaded instances and maintain their current states throughout the lifecycle of the factory.

```
public sealed class SuitFactory
{
    public enum LOADSTATUS {Ghost,Loading,Loaded};

    private static Hashtable _registered = new Hashtable();
    private static Hashtable _loaded = new Hashtable();
    private static LOADSTATUS _loadStatus = LOADSTATUS.Ghost;
```

We have two main methods in our factory. The first returns from the factory repository a stateful object instance of `Suit`. Since we are giving a reference to the object stored in the hash table collection, each reference in our static factory can be changed by multiple threads. We access all the stateful objects via the `CreateSuitWithState` method, passing in the `SuitType` enum value as a key to our `Suit` instance:

```
public static Suit CreateSuitWithState(SuitType suitType)
{
    Suit suit = null;
    if(_loaded[suitType] == null)
        Load();
    suit = (Suit)_loaded[suitType];
```

```
    if(suit != null)
        Console.WriteLine("StateFul type:" + suit.GetType().Name
            + " Enum:" + suit.TypeOfSuit + " State:"
            + suit.StateOf);
    return suit;
}
```

> **Note :** Be mindful of synchronization issues when
> writing to hash tables. If you are planning to allow
> multiple writers in .NET, you need to lock the hash table
> using the SynchRoot method. In Java you need to use
> an iterator to change the elements.

We perform a lazy load upon the call to the static
CreateSuitWithState() method to load all the registered class types. We load each registered object from the
type information we stored from the Register() method
and set each loaded object with the initialized state of
LOADSTATUS.Loaded. Notice we have the lock keyword
surrounding the code that actually loads each instance. This
is done during the load to make sure only one thread at a
time loads the objects and to prevent different threads from
overwriting each other. We also are checking the factory
status inside the lock. The first thread will see that the factory status is not loaded and will perform the load. No
other thread can access this code until the current thread
finishes executing it. Then when the next thread accesses
the code, it will see the factory is already loaded and not
perform the same load again.

```
private static void Load()
{
    lock (typeof(SuitFactory))
    {
```

```
   if(_loadStatus == LOADSTATUS.Loaded)
       return;
   _loadStatus = LOADSTATUS.Loading;
   foreach(DictionaryEntry obj in _registered)
   {
       Type type = (Type)obj.Value;
       ConstructorInfo info = type.GetConstructor(new
                           Type[]{});
       Suit suit = (Suit)info.Invoke(new object[]{});
       //if(!_loaded.ContainsKey(obj.Key))
           _loaded.Add(obj.Key,suit);


   }
   loadStatus = LOADSTATUS.Loaded;
  }
 }

}
```

The second method, `Register()`, is the method that controls workflow within our factory. We identify which class implementation types of `Suit` we wish to allow this factory instance to return. We bind the type reference with the `SuitType` enum to provide an indirect relationship between the `SuitType` enum as value type and the reflection type information. Notice we also check the factory load state and perform a load when registering new objects if the state indicates the factory is already loaded. This is done to take care of instances where the factory may be loaded already, but we wish to register a new object.

```
public static void Register(SuitType suitType, Type type)
{
    if(!_registered.ContainsKey(suitType))
    {
        _registered.Add(suitType,type);
        if(_loadStatus == LOADSTATUS.Loaded)
            Load();
```

```
        }
    }
```

When we look at the flow of the factory code, we can see how the state is changed between multiple threads accessing the same code base. We see each thread hitting the factory in turn (actually they can all hit at the same time, except for locked areas of code). As we change the state of the object, we can watch this change as it is reflected in the factory referenced object. The first call loads the object:

```
StateFul type:GolfSuit Enum:GolfSuit State:Loaded
```

We can change a value of the instance of the object and it will change the state of the object inside the factory:

```
suit.TypeOfSuit = SuitType.StripedBusinessSuit;
```

We can see the state changed:

```
StateFul type:GolfSuit Enum:StripedBusinessSuit State:Changed
```

When we next try to change the state for the same object, in this case in another thread, we get an exception:

```
StateFul type:GolfSuit Enum:StripedBusinessSuit State:Changed
--State Violation:Attribute 'TypeOfSuit' has already been modified
                  in another process and cannot be modified again
                  until the current update has been committed.
```

We can check how this works between multiple threads. Each thread that accesses an object can change the state. The changes will be reflected in every other thread. In this way we determine if an object has been changed. If it has, then we do not allow it to be changed again. Thus we maintain a factory level synchronized unit of work. We use state management to define whether or not we allow a transaction to occur.

Comparison to Similar Patterns

State patterns are related directly to any pattern that deals directly with an object's intrinsic or extrinsic state. The Memento pattern is a good example of the usage of state in how it records and restores an object's state in the memento object, stores that state in the caretaker, and restores it later to the originator. The Observer pattern also makes use of state by changing each observer's state based on changes to the subject. The Factory pattern can use state to maintain changes to shared objects it stores. The Flyweight pattern uses both intrinsic and extrinsic state to keep shared objects flyweights in a context-changeable format, allowing common state elements to be shared. Singletons maintain state as a global static property.

What We Have Learned

State is used in many other patterns to augment their functionality. State is allowed by the property of encapsulation, which governs the private nature of stateful object values and allows those values to change. State is important for sharing persistent objects in a context, or across several contexts. State acts as a point or marker of progress within a class, or signifies persistent changes within that class.

Related Patterns

- Factory pattern
- Flyweight pattern
- Memento pattern
- Observer pattern
- Singleton pattern
- Strategy pattern

Strategy Pattern

What Is a Strategy Pattern?

A *Strategy* pattern is a group of algorithms encapsulated inside classes that are made interchangeable so the algorithm can vary depending on the class used. Strategies are useful when you would like to decide at run time when to implement each algorithm. They can be used to vary each algorithm's usage by its context.

The Strategy pattern has three main components: the *Strategy*, the *Concrete Strategy*, and the *Context*. The strategy is a common interface that ties together all supported algorithms. Usually this class is abstract. The concrete strategy is the implementation class where the logic for each different algorithm lives in the group. The context is the object that ties a concrete strategy to a particular code flow.

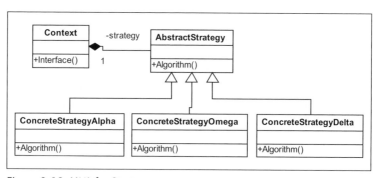

Figure 3-19. UML for Strategy pattern

Strategies are useful when you would like to use a family of algorithms across different contexts. Perhaps you have classes that each contain a different algorithm and you wish to allow them to use a common interface.

Problem: We have a series of algorithmic classes that have no correlation and are not easily exchanged but are needed to do so

For the function problem let's use an example of a set of classes that all have arithmetic code that returns a value based on the type of arithmetic you wish to perform. Each class is slightly different, but all take a common input of a value and a variance. We have a class for addition:

```
class Addition
{
    public float Add(float arithmeticValue, float arithmeticVariance)
    {
        return arithmeticValue + arithmeticVariance;
    }
}
```

And we have a class that performs subtraction on the value and variance:

```
class Subtraction
{
    public float Subtract(float arithmeticValue,
                          float arithmeticVariance)
    {
        return arithmeticValue - arithmeticVariance;
    }
}
```

When we use each one we have to make the class part of the compile-time logic. We allow user input to decide which

Behavioral Patterns

algorithm to use at any given time. Right now we have `if...then...else` code to do this, but it is not very efficient. If we wanted to add a class to perform multiplication and a class to perform division, we would have to add to or change the `if...then...else` code for each algorithm.

```
If(DoAdd)
    Addition calc = new Addition();
    calc.Add(12,7);
else
    Subtraction calc = new Subtraction();
    calc.Subtract(12,7);
```

We need a better and more flexible way to add classes and manage the algorithmic grouping. We need to use a common interface that ties all these classes together as well. Below, we see the two new classes we wish to add. There is one to perform multiplication on the value and variance and one to perform division:

```
class Multiplication
{
    public float Multiply(float arithmeticValue,
                          float arithmeticVariance)
    {
        return arithmeticValue * arithmeticVariance;
    }
}
class Division
{
    public float Divide(float arithmeticValue,
                        float arithmeticVariance)
    {
        return arithmeticValue / arithmeticVariance;
    }
}
```

Solution: Make each class inherit from a common base to provide ease of scalability and exchange between class types so one algorithm class can easily be exchanged for another

To solve this technical problem we will employ the Strategy pattern to help us write streamlined code. We use the Strategy pattern in this case because we are using a family of algorithms that all have similar input.

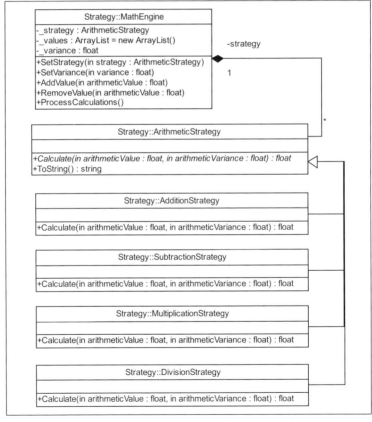

Figure 3-20. UML for Strategy pattern example

The first step in refactoring to the pattern is to create the common interface between all these classes, the strategy. This abstract class defines the basic interface that all the implementation classes use to define their particular equation. Notice the method `Calculate()`. This method is marked as abstract, and will be used by the implementation classes to contain each different strategy's algorithm.

```
abstract class ArithmeticStrategy
{
    public abstract float Calculate(
        float arithmeticValue,
        float arithmeticVariance);
}
```

The next step in refactoring to the pattern is to build each implementation class. These classes will inherit from the base class `ArithmeticStrategy`. Each class will override the method `Calculate()` and provide its own calculation algorithm. Below, we see the first strategy. Notice that it returns the correct type for the method, but the calculation it uses to return the value is specialized to this strategy.

```
class AdditionStrategy : ArithmeticStrategy
{
    public override float Calculate(
        float arithmeticValue,
        float arithmeticVariance)
    {
        return arithmeticValue + arithmeticVariance;
    }
}
```

As we build our other strategies, we will use the particular logic that resides in the original classes to implement the correct algorithm:

```
class SubtractionStrategy : ArithmeticStrategy
{
    public override float Calculate(
        float arithmeticValue,
        float arithmeticVariance)
    {
        return arithmeticValue - arithmeticVariance;
    }
}

class MultiplicationStrategy : ArithmeticStrategy
{
    public override float Calculate(
        float arithmeticValue,
        float arithmeticVariance)
    {
        return arithmeticValue * arithmeticVariance;
    }
}

class DivisionStrategy : ArithmeticStrategy
{
    public override float Calculate(
        float arithmeticValue,
        float arithmeticVariance)
    {
        return arithmeticValue / arithmeticVariance;
    }
}
```

Now that we have created all our strategy classes, we need to create an object to deal with the strategy we want to use for each situation. We will call this object the Context object. It is thus named since it will be the point in code where an action occurs. This object will house the strategy object for its instance, all the values to which to apply the strategy, and a variance to apply to the values based on the strategy algorithm:

```
class MathEngine
{
    ......

    public void SetStrategy(ArithmeticStrategy strategy)
    {
        _strategy = strategy;
    }
    public void SetVariance(float variance)
    {
        _variance = variance;
    }

    public void AddValue(float arithmeticValue)
    {
        _values.Add(arithmeticValue);
    }

    public void RemoveValue(float arithmeticValue)
    {
        _values.Remove(arithmeticValue);
    }
```

We also have a method to process all the values using the variance and the strategy to be used for this context instance:

```
public void ProcessCalculations()
{
    foreach(float val in _values)
        Console.WriteLine("{0} uses {1} and variance {2}
                          for result:{3}",
            _strategy,val,_variance,_
                strategy.Calculate(val,_variance));
}
}
```

Last, we will implement the context with a particular strategy. We will instantiate our context object and add some values that we want to process to the context:

```
MathEngine engine = new MathEngine();
engine.AddValue(15);
engine.AddValue(3);
engine.AddValue(8);
engine.AddValue(100);
engine.AddValue(55);
```

For each strategy algorithm we set our variance that the input values will calculate against:

```
engine.SetVariance(20);
```

Next, we need to add the strategy containing the algorithm we would like to use to process our values against our variance with the context object:

```
engine.SetStrategy(new AdditionStrategy());
```

Now we call the method used to process each value:

```
engine.ProcessCalculations();
```

And we can see our results for each application of the algorithm from the strategy we chose:

```
AdditionStrategy uses 15 and variance 20 for result:35
AdditionStrategy uses 3 and variance 20 for result:23
AdditionStrategy uses 8 and variance 20 for result:28
AdditionStrategy uses 100 and variance 20 for result:120
AdditionStrategy uses 55 and variance 20 for result:75
```

We can continue by setting the strategy to a new type and running the process method again as many times as needed. Notice the values will change depending on the strategy used each time we run the process method:

```
engine.SetStrategy(new SubtractionStrategy());
engine.ProcessCalculations();
......
SubtractionStrategy uses 15 and variance 20 for result:-5
SubtractionStrategy uses 3 and variance 20 for result:-17
SubtractionStrategy uses 8 and variance 20 for result:-12
SubtractionStrategy uses 100 and variance 20 for result:80
SubtractionStrategy uses 55 and variance 20 for result:35
......
engine.SetStrategy(new MultiplicationStrategy());
engine.ProcessCalculations();
......
MultiplicationStrategy uses 15 and variance 20 for result:300
MultiplicationStrategy uses 3 and variance 20 for result:60
MultiplicationStrategy uses 8 and variance 20 for result:160
MultiplicationStrategy uses 100 and variance 20 for result:2000
MultiplicationStrategy uses 55 and variance 20 for result:1100
......
engine.SetStrategy(new DivisionStrategy());
engine.ProcessCalculations();
......
DivisionStrategy uses 15 and variance 20 for result:0.75
DivisionStrategy uses 3 and variance 20 for result:0.15
DivisionStrategy uses 8 and variance 20 for result:0.4
DivisionStrategy uses 100 and variance 20 for result:5
DivisionStrategy uses 55 and variance 20 for result:2.75
```

Comparison to Similar Patterns

Strategies give us an interesting way to deal with grouping algorithmic equations. If we look at the Flyweight pattern, we see that this pattern uses a type of strategy method but also pools these strategies in a central repository or factory. Each flyweight has its own implementation of methods and intrinsic and extrinsic states, each of which could be thought of as algorithms. The Template pattern utilizes the abstraction of strategies to allow common interfaces among different algorithms. State is maintained on the context object in the form of the setting of values, variances, and strategies inside this object.

What We Have Learned

Strategies are useful ways to maintain a family of algorithms in such a way that they can easily be called dynamically and independent of immutable logical code. They allow similar inputs to interact in different ways just by switching the strategy type. Expressions can change by swapping only the strategy, not the inputs, giving flexibility to interfaces that may receive inputs from different sources that need processing in a unified manner.

Related Patterns

- Flyweight pattern
- State pattern
- Template pattern

Template Pattern

What Is a Template Pattern?

The *Template* pattern is the definition of the relationship abstract classes have to their inherited members. This pattern defines the skeleton or template for a group of classes as a parent class, and allows inherited members to modify this template without changing the underlying template class.

The Template pattern has two components: the *Template* class and the *Concrete* class. The template is the base or abstract class that acts as the skeleton for all the shared functionality that gets inherited to the class instances, or concrete classes. Each concrete class can override the methods and functions of the template class or use these inherited methods without overriding them.

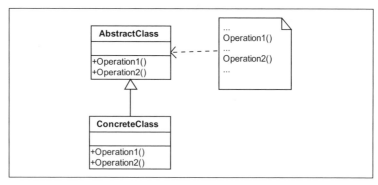

Figure 3-21. UML for Template pattern

This pattern is the basic model for all inheritance of classes. Although the GoF doesn't say this directly, there are a couple of good rules to follow with this pattern. One is to limit the layers of inheritance to no deeper than two layers. This is to prevent overcomplication of your code by using too many inherited classes. If you find you need a variety of functionality for inherited members, and some inherited classes share this functionality and some do not need to, you might try a plug-and-play pattern like the Visitor pattern. The Visitor pattern gives a little more flexibility to add new functionality without using multiple layers of direct inheritance and without rewriting this functionality in the new members. This allows the sharing of functionality across classes, without the need for deep and complicated inherited members.

Problem: Shared functionality between classes is desired without copying functionality

For our functional problem, we have two classes that we would like to use as template classes. We would like to share some functionality between these base classes and inherited members, but not share all the specialized logic inside these members. The classes are called Document and Application:

```
class Document
{
    public Document(string path){...}

    public string FilePath{...}

    public void Create(){...}
    public void Open(FileMode mode, FileAccess access) {...}
    public void Close(){...}
```

Behavioral Patterns

```
    public object Read(){...}
    public void Write(object writeable) {...}
}

class Application
{
    public Document OpenDocument(string path) {...}
    public bool CanOpenDocument(string path) {...}
    public Document CreateDocument(string path) {...}
}
```

The `Document` class is used inside the `Application` class. Both classes have specialized logic inside their methods. Some of these methods we would like to share as templates with inherited members, but we do not want the specialized logic from every method. We would like to share the method templates without inheriting the logic inside those methods. We would also like some functionality to be shared among all the inherited members.

Solution: Make both classes inherit from a single base that contains shared functionality

Our solution to our functional problem is to first make our two classes abstract. The methods that will contain only the core functional logic that needs to be shared will be marked virtual. The other methods we will use as templates are made abstract so we can have the inherited members define the logic in their override of these methods. As the following shows, we have made the `Document` and `Application` classes abstract so that they become the template for the pattern:

```
abstract class Application
{

    public abstract Document OpenDocument(string path);
    public virtual bool CanOpenDocument(string path) {...}
    public abstract Document CreateDocument(string path);
}

abstract class Document
{
    public Document(string path) {...}

    public string FilePath {...}

    public abstract void Create();
    protected abstract void Open(FileMode mode, FileAccess access);
    protected abstract void Close();
    public abstract object Read();
    public abstract void Write(object writeable);
}
```

We have the functional logic that is not specialized still located in the virtual methods and private variables. This will allow all inherited members to share this functionality. For the methods that are specialized to the inherited members, we will override them and prepare this logic in the methods of the inherited members.

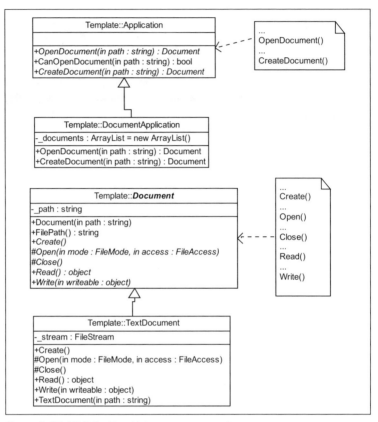

Figure 3-22. UML for Template pattern example

For our purposes we have created two new inherited members that can be instantiated, one for each class. For the Document class, which is now abstract and cannot be instantiated, we have created the TextDocument class. This class overrides the Document class and allows specialization of the type of document we wish to use.

```
class TextDocument : Document
{
    public TextDocument(string path) : base(path){}
```

Notice in the overridden method `Create()` that we are adding specialized logic on how to create a text type of file. If we wanted to create a byte file, we could inherit another class and change the logic to meet those needs.

```
public override void Create()
{
    _stream = File.Open(FilePath, FileMode.Create,
                        FileAccess.ReadWrite);
    _stream.Close();
}
```

With the other members of the `Document` class we include the specialized code for this instance type. This allows us to build similar class instances that can all be used interchangeably, but each performs its job differently.

```
protected override void Open(FileMode mode, FileAccess access)
{
    _stream = File.Open(FilePath, mode, access);
}
protected override void Close()
{
    _stream.Close();
}
public override object Read()
{
    object readable = null;
    Open(FileMode.Open, FileAccess.Read);
    using (StreamReader sr = new StreamReader(_stream))
    {
        String line;
        // Read and display lines from the file until the end
        // of the file is reached.
        while ((line = sr.ReadLine()) != null)
        {
            readable += " - " + line;
            Console.WriteLine(line);
        }
```

Behavioral Patterns

```
                sr.Close();
        }
        return readable;
    }

    public override void Write(object writeable)
    {
        Open(FileMode.Append, FileAccess.Write);
        using(StreamWriter sw = new StreamWriter(_stream))
        {
            sw.WriteLine(writeable);
            sw.Close();
        }
    }
}
```

The `Application` class works in a similar fashion. We
override this class to keep it as a template, keeping the
shared functionality in the base class. In the inherited class,
we keep an array of documents that we can manipulate. We
also define how we will deal with a particular document
type.

```
class DocumentApplication : Application
{
    private ArrayList _documents = new ArrayList();

    public override Document OpenDocument(string path)
    {
        if(!CanOpenDocument(path)) return null;
        Document document = new TextDocument(path);
        _documents.Add(document);
        return document;
    }

    public override Document CreateDocument(string path)
    {
        if(CanOpenDocument(path)) return null;
        Document document = new TextDocument(path);
```

```
        document.Create();
        _documents.Add(document);
        return document;
    }
}
```

Now when we load the `Application` object, we specify the object type as the implementation class we want. From this class we have defined the `Document` object type as `TextDocument`. This allows the `Application` object to specify the type of `Document` object we wish to return by the `Application` object's type:

```
DocumentApplication application = new DocumentApplication();
Document doc = application.CreateDocument(path);
```

Since this `Application` class type creates a text document, we can write text to it:

```
doc.Write("This is a Test!");
doc.Write("This is another Test!");
```

We can also call the created document from the `Application` class and do something to it directly:

```
Document docReopened = application.OpenDocument(path);

docReopened.Write("This is the 2nd Test!");
docReopened.Write("This is another 2nd Test!");

docReopened.Read();
```

We could define other implementation classes now, using the same `Document` and `Application` classes as templates. Each implementation can define the overridden methods for a different application or document type.

Comparison to Similar Patterns

The Template pattern is related to almost all the other patterns in some fashion. Since it defines the relationship between a parent class and its inherited members, the Template pattern can be seen in usage with most of the other patterns in some way.

What We Have Learned

The Template pattern gives us the very basic and useful relationship definition between a parent class and all its subclasses. It allows us to establish the inherited relationship for sharing and defining class structures, for use in polymorphic transitions in class types at run time or in code flow.

Related Patterns

- Abstract Factory pattern
- Adapter pattern
- Bridge pattern
- Builder pattern
- Chain of Responsibility pattern
- Command pattern
- Factory pattern
- Flyweight pattern
- Mediator pattern
- Observer pattern
- Prototype pattern
- Strategy pattern
- Visitor pattern

Visitor Pattern

What Is a Visitor Pattern?

The *Visitor* pattern allows changes or additions to a class's structure without changing the actual class. The pattern allows this by passing into a class other classes with the same method structure but different functionality, and using that passed-in class's method to change the class's behavior. In other words, instead of coding methods or algorithms that perform functions inside a class, we pass in references to other classes that have the desired functionality. Then we allow the methods and algorithms on the passed-in classes to influence the behavior of the class we wish to modify.

This pattern has several components. The *Visitor* is the abstract base for the implementation classes that contain the functional methods. The *Concrete Visitor* contains the actual functional method and controls which *Element* type is allowed to use this method. The element is the abstract base for the class that actually contains the state we wish to modify. The implementation or instance of this class in the pattern is known as the concrete element. The *Object Structure* provides a container that allows an enumeration of the different element classes that we will allow the visitors to interact with.

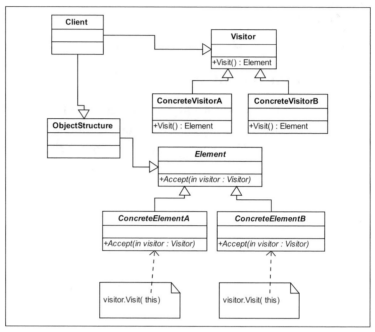

Figure 3-23. UML for Visitor pattern

To understand the usefulness of the pattern let's examine a functional example. Suppose you wanted to perform a certain function on a class's attribute. However, the functional method you wish to use exists in another class. You don't wish to provide an uncontrolled usage of that method, and you would not really want to rewrite the method in the class where you want to modify the attribute. And for clarity or for some other reason, you don't wish to inherit from the class with that method. So to accomplish this using the method on the other class that modifies your class's attributes, you would need to somehow share this method in an efficient manner.

This is where the Visitor pattern can come in handy. Allowing the functional method to be housed in the Visitor class allows a separation of duties between the class that needs this functionality and the actual function. When needed, the visitor can be passed to the element and the element can then submit itself to the visitor method, allowing the visitor implementation class passed to determine which functionality will be used to modify the attributes (or state) of the host element object. Thus, the element class does not need to be modified to change its attributes (or state), only a different visitor needs to be passed in. If you needed a series of elements to be changed by your visitor, you use the object structure object to house and provide a single interface for all your element objects. The object structure object contains a series of elements and, when a visitor is passed in, it iterates through each element, allowing the visitor to interact with each element object.

Let's now look at some actual problems with code and how the visitor can assist us in better implementations refactored from Boolean logic.

Problem: We have a need for a class that encapsulates database transactions and performs specific functions based on the class instance type

Our functional problem is one that you may not encounter all that often, but when you do it can be quite frustrating to figure out without using a pattern. Although we could use other patterns to accomplish the same goal, the Visitor pattern seems to be a particularly good one for this example.

We start out with the class `Customer`. The `Customer` class accepts the name of the customer and the customer's initial total. It also has two other methods that are notable, `Credit()` and `Debit()`, which do pretty much what they imply.

```
class Customer : Element
{
    public Customer(string name, double balance){...}

    public string Name{...}

    public double Balance{...}

    public void Credit(double amount)
    {
        _balance += amount;
    }

    public void Debit(double amount)
    {
        _balance -= amount;
    }
}
```

To credit or debit a customer we currently rely on a Boolean statement to identify what type of processing we wish to accomplish. This has worked for a while, but now we would like to encapsulate the database preprocessing and the change of the customer balance. Also, we would like to call several customers in a single transaction and have a single point to manage these customers. Below we see a snippet of the code we wish to refactor:

```
//transaction code
Customer customer = new Customer(customerName,balanceTotal);

//DB is our data layer
```

```
if(amount > 0)
    customer.Credit(DB.Credit(amount));
else
    customer.Debit(DB.Debit(amount));
//end transaction code
```

To perform the data processing (a database call to send the credit or debit), we accomplish this before the call to the methods `Credit()` and `Debit()`. Right now we cannot easily encapsulate this data-processing code or change it without rewriting the inline code. We would like a way to encapsulate both of the preprocessing methods and change the customer object's state to reflect what we are sending to the database. We would also like to allow changing of multiple customers inside a transaction and have that handled from a single point. And lastly, we would like to be able to change which kind of data processing we perform without specifying the actual method needed or linking it to the customer object until it is needed at run time.

Solution: Place each database transaction type in a class that controls that functionality, and use this class to send the data into the database

The first part of our solution is to define the abstract base classes for `Element` and `Visitor`. The base classes give us a way to link all the other concrete classes together and limit usage to only these accepted types. So, for instance, an element for another type could not be passed into the visitor's methods, because only types of `Element` can be used. This limits the scope and helps to define the logic in a more comprehensive manner. Defining this helps solve our problem of encapsulation for our credit and debit processing by setting the abstract methods as templates.

Behavioral Patterns

```
abstract class Visitor
{
    public abstract void Visit(Element element);
}

abstract class Element
{
    public abstract void Accept(Visitor visitor);
}
```

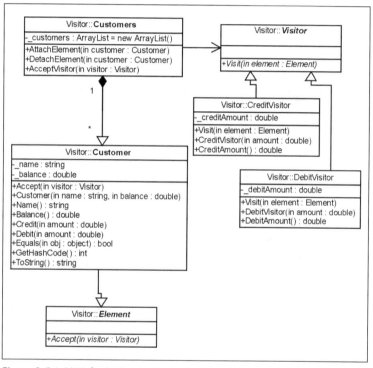

Figure 3-24. UML for Visitor pattern example

The second part of our solution is to place the actual data processing and modification of the customer balance inside the concrete visitor. We will need to refactor the data processing and customer object's balance modification from the Boolean logic code into an acceptable method inside a different concrete visitor class for the credit and debit.

So we will move the logic we are seeing in the example in the problem section for credit and debit of the customer object to the Visit() method of two concrete visitor classes, CreditVisitor and DebitVisitor. This solves our encapsulation needs for the data processing and modification of the customer's balance.

```
class CreditVisitor : Visitor
{
    public CreditVisitor(double amount){...}

    public override void Visit(Element element)
    {
        Customer customer = (Customer)element;
        customer.Credit(DB.Credit(amount));
    }
}
class DebitVisitor : Visitor
{
    public DebitVisitor(double amount) {...}

    public override void Visit(Element element)
    {
        Customer customer = (Customer)element;
        customer.Debit(DB.Debit(amount));
    }
}
```

Next we define the concrete element. We will allow the Customer object to inherit from the Element base class.

This ensures that only accepted types can be passed into the visitor's `Visit()` method.

```
class Customer : Element
{    ...    }
```

Last, we want to define our object structure class object. This is the object that will allow us to apply the concrete visitor's method to a series of customers without having to send them through one at time. We have three major methods on this class: `AttachElement()`, `Detach-Element()`, and `AcceptVisitor()`. `Attach-Element()` allows us to add a customer to the enumeration of `Customers`. `DetachElement()` removes `Customers` from the enumeration. The `Accept-Visitor()` method allows application of the visitor method to multiple customers inside a transaction.

```
class Customers
{
    public void AttachElement(Customer customer)
    {
        _customers.Add(customer);
    }

    public void DetachElement(Customer customer)
    {
        _customers.Remove(customer);
    }

    public void AcceptVisitor(Visitor visitor)
    {
        foreach(Customer customer in _customers)
            customer.Accept(visitor);
    }
}
```

Now we can look at how we call the pattern code and make use of it inside the transaction.

First, we need to instantiate our `Customers` collection that we will use to apply our visitor to:

```
//transaction code
Customers customers = new Customers();
```

Next, we need to attach our `Customer` classes to the collection. This will allow the collection to apply the visitor method to each customer registered with the collection. Notice each customer class has a name and balance as input parameters:

```
customers.AttachElement(new Customer("George",233.50));
customers.AttachElement(new Customer("Janice",102.25));
customers.AttachElement(new Customer("Richard",2005.48));
```

Now we can create our visitor classes. We instantiate them with the values they will use to modify each customer:

```
CreditVisitor creditVisitor = new CreditVisitor(50.15);
DebitVisitor debitVisitor = new DebitVisitor(22.20);
```

Then we call our `AcceptVisitor` method, which will loop through the `Customers` collection and apply the `Accept()` method to each customer. Remember, the algorithm in each visitor class's `Visit()` method performs a specific function. The credit visitor performs a credit in the database and returns the balance:

```
customers.AcceptVisitor(creditVisitor);
and the resulting values:
------------------------------
Accepting CreditVisitor
CreditVisitor credited George $50.15. Balance:283.65
CreditVisitor credited Janice $50.15. Balance:152.4
CreditVisitor credited Richard $50.15. Balance:2055.63
```

While the debit visitor performs a debit in the database:

```
customers.AcceptVisitor(debitVisitor);
```

and returns the result:

```
-----------------------------
Accepting DebitVisitor
DebitVisitor debited George $22.2. Balance:261.45
DebitVisitor debited Janice $22.2. Balance:130.2
DebitVisitor debited Richard $22.2. Balance:2033.43
```

Comparison to Similar Patterns

The Visitor pattern is similar to the Decorator pattern in that we use classes to pass and encapsulate functionality, and we share that functionality depending on the particular implementation. There is also a bit of similarity between this pattern and the Composite pattern, since composites add functions to a class instance at run time.

What We Have Learned

The Visitor pattern allows us some flexibility on how we wish to allow sharing of functionality. It gives us this flexibility through a looser association than direct class inheritance, and allows us to change the implementation of class methods at run time instead of at compile time as with class inheritance. By simply changing a type, we can change the function that is associated with either a single class or collections of classes.

Related Patterns

- Adapter pattern
- Composite pattern
- Decorator pattern
- Template pattern

4

Structural Patterns

Structural patterns are patterns whose sole purpose is to facilitate the work of changing the structural associations of classes, class associations, and hierarchies of class structures. Most structural patterns take on the form of facades or types of proxies and adapters. There is one exception to this — the Flyweight pattern. This pattern is also a structural pattern in that it provides an adaptation of sorts, albeit a disjointed one. Since it does have the definition of changing the structural association of classes in the form of shared instances as opposed to individual ones, it is included with this group of patterns. We will discuss the Flyweight pattern later in the chapter. For now we will concentrate on patterns like the Adapter pattern, which is a more solid example of a structural pattern.

Adapter Pattern

What Is an Adapter Pattern?

The *Adapter* pattern is a useful pattern for making two different class types communicate in a similar manner. It performs much as its name implies: it creates an adaptation between two classes of different types so they can become interchangeable.

The Adapter pattern has three important components: the *Target*, *Adapter*, and *Adaptee*. The target is the class for which we wish to implement the adapter. We inherit from the target to create our adapter. The adapter is the class that provides the join for the two disparate class types and houses the methods for conjoining functionality between them. It is an inherited member from the target. The adaptee is the class that we wish to give access to the methods and functionality of the target. The adapter allows interchangeability between the target and the adaptee.

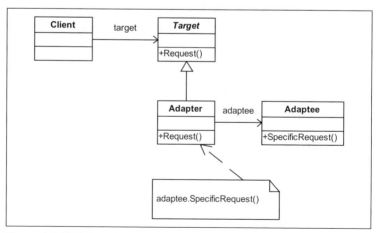

Figure 4-1. UML for Adapter pattern

This seems to be a simple enough pattern. It can also be quite useful when dealing with incompatible class types in a class solution where it is desired that neither class have any real association directly with the other, but that they use similar methods. In other words, the adapter allows the target to perform normally on the outside but inside it will actually use the adaptee's methods and functionality.

Problem: We wish to allow one class to use another's methods without using direct inheritance

For our functional problem I have chosen a simple equation. I have a class named `Water`, which houses some basic functions to manipulate temperature limits for different levels of heat:

```
//Adaptee
class Water
{
    public void SetBoilingTemperature(float temperature)
    {
        .....

    }
    public void SetIceTemperature(float temperature)
    {
        .....

    }
    public void SetLiquidTemperature(float temperature)
    {
        .....

    }
}
```

Structural Patterns

Notice each method takes a `float` that signifies temperature. Our methods could be anything; the important detail is that we wish to share these methods with other class types without modifying the class itself or the classes with which we wish to share functionality. Let's say for this example we have a class named `Element`, which would also like to take advantage of the `Water` class's methods:

```
class Element
{
.....

    public virtual void SetVaporTemperature(float temperature)
    {
        .....
    }
    public virtual void SetFreezeTemperature(float temperature)
    {
        .....
    }
    public virtual void SetNormalTemperature(float temperature)
    {
        .....
    }
}
```

We don't want to use inheritance between each class for some reason, probably to enforce the domain-specific rules of the `Element` class, the `Water` class, or both. Yet sometimes we wish to let `Element` act as though it were `Water`, although it does not directly access `Water` through inheritance or direct association. We can see that `Element` and `Water` both have similar methods, but that they are basically different:

```
Element silicon = new Element("Silicon");
silicon.SetFreezeTemperature(-20);
silicon.SetVaporTemperature(3000);
silicon.SetNormalTemperature(105);

Water water = new Water();
water.SetIceTemperature(20);
water.SetLiquidTemperature(75);
water.SetBoilingTemperature(140);
```

To use them interchangeably at this point we would have to change one or both classes, or provide some Boolean method such as:

```
if(some condition)
{
    Element silicon = new Element("Silicon");
    silicon.SetFreezeTemperature(-20);
    silicon.SetVaporTemperature(3000);
    silicon.SetNormalTemperature(105);
}
else (some other condition)
{
    Water water = new Water();
    water.SetIceTemperature(20);
    water.SetLiquidTemperature(75);
    water.SetBoilingTemperature(140);
}
```

For many reasons we might not want to do this. Probably the most notable is the lack of any polymorphic aspect between the two classes.

Solution: Allow an adapter class to hold an instance of the desired class and adapt its methods, properties, and events through the adapter's methods, properties, and events

The solution we will use for this particular problem is to create an adapter class that can allow the `Element` to act using the `Water` class's methods. Our adapter will inherit from `Element` and will encapsulate `Water` as a private instance variable.

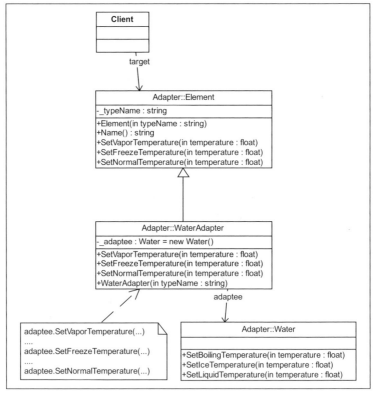

Figure 4-2. UML for Adapter pattern example

Doing this allows the adapter, which we will call the WaterAdapter class, to house and connect the Water class's methods directly into the overridden methods of the Element class. So now when we instantiate the Element class as an instance of WaterAdapter, we are actually calling the encapsulated Water class's methods as the adaptee:

```
//Adapter
class WaterAdapter : Element
{
    private Water _adaptee = new Water();

    public WaterAdapter(string typeName) : base (typeName){}

    public override void SetVaporTemperature(float temperature)
    {
        _adaptee.SetBoilingTemperature(temperature);
    }
    public override void SetFreezeTemperature(float temperature)
    {
        _adaptee.SetIceTemperature(temperature);
    }
    public override void SetNormalTemperature(float temperature)
    {
        _adaptee.SetLiquidTemperature(temperature);
    }
}
```

Now we have the option to call the Element class as before, but with one difference. We can now call the Element class as the WaterAdapter, and use the polymorphic qualities of the two classes to determine whether we wish to use the base element's functions of its adaptee class Water functions:

```
Element silicon = new Element("Silicon");
silicon.SetFreezeTemperature(-20);
```

Structural Patterns

```
silicon.SetVaporTemperature(3000);
silicon.SetNormalTemperature(105);

Element water = new WaterAdapter("H20");
water.SetFreezeTemperature(20);
water.SetVaporTemperature(140);
water.SetNormalTemperature(75);
```

Comparison to Similar Patterns

The Adapter pattern has similarities to some other structural patterns like Bridge and Proxy, but also has some similarities to the Visitor pattern. Its similarities to the first two patterns may be obvious in that it acts as an intermediary between two class or domain areas that are themselves immutable. Its similarities to the latter pattern are in its ability to exchange functionality depending on the adaptee that is implemented, much like the Visitor pattern exchanges functionality between classes based on type.

What We Have Learned

The Adapter pattern gives us a way to provide a more common connection between uncommon class structures. If you have one class that is dissimilar to other classes you wish to emulate, you can use an adapter class to make the foreign class appear and function as the accepted type, at least in some ways. By adapting the methods, properties, or events of a class through the adapter, you can make inexact class structures work as if they were inherited from the same base. This is especially important when you wish to have different classes appear to be inheriting from the same base, without rewriting either the class to be adapted or the class for which you wish to adapt.

Related Patterns

- Bridge pattern
- Decorator pattern
- Facade pattern
- Proxy pattern
- Template pattern
- Visitor pattern

Structural Patterns

Bridge Pattern

What Is a Bridge Pattern?

Another instance of where simple inheritance cannot meet the immediate needs of the programmer is one where abstraction is not desired. When you use abstraction or inheritance, you are tied to the exact definition of that abstraction. Sometimes you would like this to be more flexible. Some cases would require classes to not be inherited, but instead we would like to adapt other classes to act as the desired type without modifying either class.

Usually an Adapter pattern would suffice to join different class types when inheritance is not desired. However, in some cases the actual implementation of the adapter needs to be more flexible. It is then that the adapter's cousin, the *Bridge* pattern, comes into play. As we saw in the "Adapter Pattern" section, the adapter houses an instance variable of the desired type to adapt as an intrinsic variable, or a private instance variable. This instance variable is not changeable in the class. This means it is not set as an abstract or base variable but as a concrete type. We hide this instance variable's methods, properties, and events behind overridden methods, properties, and events matching the adapter's base, thus making it compatible with the expected class type the adapter is inheriting.

In the Bridge pattern we expand on this, allowing the instance variable to be not a concrete type but an abstract type, thus giving us a variance on which class we wish to adapt, or bridge. We still inherit the bridge from the expected base type and override the methods, properties, and events of that type. The difference here is that we are dependent on which concrete implementation of the abstract instance inside the bridge we have selected. Let's talk about the actual parts of the pattern and then we can find out more about this in detail.

The Bridge pattern has four main parts. The first is the *Abstraction*, which is the base for the bridge that holds the abstracted instance variable for the class to be adapted. The next part is the *Refined Abstraction*, which is the concrete implementation of the abstracted bridge. This part of the pattern is where we define the methods, properties, and events for which we wish to provide a bridge. The other half of the pattern is the *Abstract Implementor* and the *Concrete Implementor*. These two classes define the abstraction and concrete interface for the class for which we wish to bridge into the new type. The abstract implementor is the abstract instance variable to be set as the concrete implementor type at run time.

So in short, we provide a way to encapsulate a desired implementation of a class from which we do not wish to inherit. We provide methods, properties, and events in the concrete bridge based on another base type. We encapsulate the methods, properties, and events of the desired implementation class inside the bridged methods, properties, and events. The instance of the internal abstract implementation is interchangeable because of its abstract status. This allows not only polymorphism of the bridge, but also of the desired encapsulated instance implementation class inside the bridge.

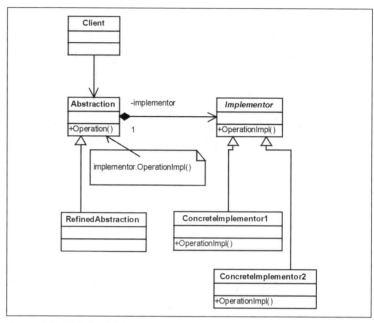

Figure 4-3. UML for Bridge pattern

Problem: We need to allow a class to use functionality from a series of class types without using direct inheritance

For our functional problem, we have a class that has a single method and inherits a base. This is a good starting point for making a bridge, because we can easily refactor the base class to be our bridge's abstraction to hold our implementor. We have an instance where our implementor is another class type that we do not want to inherit, probably because the methods do not match exactly. This is usually the case when using a bridge. You have two class types that have similar functionality, but the method, property, or event names, input parameters, etc., are slightly different. We call this an *inexact match*. Inexact matches occur when two class types are similar but not enough so for the compiler to recognize. This is a good case for refactoring into a bridge, as opposed to inheriting directly.

Below we see our implementor class types. Notice the method `ProcessRequest()`. This method, as we will see in our next code example, is mirrored in the bridge class, but with a slightly different name. For this example, we don't want to change any method names, and because of that the two class types cannot inherit directly. The reason for this is that compilers require that method names match in inherited instances.

```
class HttpRequest
{
    public override void ProcessRequest(string request)
    {
        .......
    }
}
class ISAPIRequest
{
    public override void ProcessRequest(string request)
    {
        .......
    }
}
```

Here we see the class we have targeted to turn into our bridge. Notice this class has a method similar to the implementation class but named differently. For this example, the method's internal functionality is similar, and so meets the requirements of the Bridge pattern:

```
class RequestHandler : Request
{
    public override void Process(string request)
    {
```

```
        //some implementation code
    }
}
```

What we wish to do is to make the `RequestHandler` class use our implementor handler types, without the overhead of actual inheritance from these types. Next, we will see how we can accomplish this and not have direct inheritance using the `RequestHandler` class as a bridge.

Solution: Create a series of classes and allow a bridge class to hold the desired instance of the series and adapt its methods, properties, and events through the bridge's methods, properties, and events

The first step after deciding to use the pattern in our refactoring effort is to identify the classes that we wish to make implementors and the classes that will act as the bridge. Since we have done this in our problem section, we will start by refactoring our implementors. This is usually not a difficult task, as they only need to inherit from a common base.

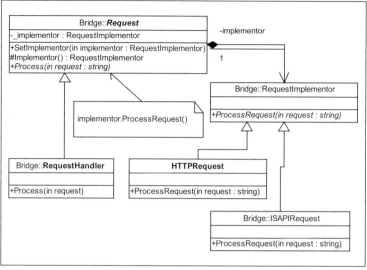

Figure 4-4. UML for Bridge pattern example

Below, we add a base and make both implementors inherit from that base. This allows for the concrete instance, which we will house inside the bridge class. We provide an abstract method for inherited types to share: `Process-Request()`. This enables this method to be called from any concrete instance we select inside our bridge.

```
abstract class RequestImplementor
{
    public abstract void ProcessRequest(string request);
}
```

Next, we refactor our implementor classes to have the abstract `RequestImplementor` class as their base. We override the `RequestImplementor` class's abstract method `ProcessRequest()`, which gives us our polymorphic implementation:

```
class HttpRequest : RequestImplementor
{
    public override void ProcessRequest(string request)
    {
        ......
    }
}
class ISAPIRequest : RequestImplementor
{
    public override void ProcessRequest(string request)
    {
        ......
    }
}
```

Next we need to refactor our bridge's base class. We have determined that the Request class is a good case for this. We provide a private instance variable for the abstract implementor. We provide a *getter* and a way to set the actual concrete implementation of our abstract implementor to the instance variable. We also provide an abstract method, Process(), which will be used to allow the inherited instances of Request to have a common method. This method is refactored from the original method.

```
abstract class Request
{
    private RequestImplementor _implementor;

    public void SetImplementor(RequestImplementor implementor)
    {
        _implementor = implementor;
    }

    protected RequestImplementor Implementor
    {
        get{return _implementor;}
    }
```

```
    public abstract void Process(string request);

}
```

In `Request`'s inherited classes we will then override the
`Process()` method. Inside the method we will call the
instance class of the implementor and pass our arguments
from the `Process()` method to the implementor's desired
method to bridge to — `ProcessRequest()`:

```
//Refined Abstraction
class RequestHandler : Request
{
    public override void Process(string request)
    {
        Implementor.ProcessRequest(request);
    }
}
```

Thus we have performed a complete refactoring of the
implementor into our bridge class without using direct
inheritance. Now we can call our bridge, set the desired
implementor, and call the `Process()` method, which calls
the implementor's intrinsic method `ProcessRequest()`.
This gives us a complete bridge between classes without the
need for any direct inheritance.

```
Request request = new RequestHandler();
request.SetImplementor(new HttpRequest());
request.Process("This is a HTTP request stream..");

request.SetImplementor(new ISAPIRequest());
request.Process("This is a ISAPI request stream..");
```

Structural Patterns

Comparison to Similar Patterns

The Adapter pattern is most like the Bridge pattern, in that it uses a host class or facade class to house an instance of the actual desired class, calling the housed methods, properties, and events and hiding these events inside the corresponding methods, properties, and events that exist as public methods for the adapter. The main difference in the two patterns is the adapter's lack of abstraction and inheritance in regard to its internal implementation and the outside adapter. A Bridge pattern might be more useful if several different types of classes or implementations are required for a particular problem. Proxies and facades are also very similar to bridges in that they house some functionality that external sources could not use easily. They basically act as an interface or adapter for subsets of functionality, expanding on the control of the scope and domain from a single class or class type as in the bridge and adapter to more complex subsets of classes and expanded domains.

What We Have Learned

The Bridge pattern is a useful pattern for making slightly incompatible classes and their subclasses more compatible. It gives us a way to do this without using inheritance and by minimizing the abstracted functionality between classes to expected methods, properties, and events. It takes a series of abstracted class types and adapts their functionality to another series of unrelated classes with a minimum of actual cohesion between the two class structures, while providing all the functionality between the two classes that is desired.

Related Patterns

- Adapter pattern
- Facade pattern
- Proxy pattern
- Template pattern

Composite Pattern

What Is a Composite Pattern?

The *Composite* pattern is a collection pattern that allows you to compound different subsets of functionality into a collection and then call each subset in turn in the collection at a given point.

Let's say you had a collection of objects, and each object had a particular method that you wanted to call in series. You could call each method in the collection separately, but this would take time and a lot of code:

```
obj1.Operation();
obj2.Operation();
obj3.Operation();
obj4.Operation();
obj5.Operation();
obj6.Operation();
obj7.Operation();
...... and so on
```

Instead, a composite allows you to call the classes with a single method and loop through the collection, calling the method on each class. This remains flexible because each class in the collection as well as the collection class itself all derive from the same base class. We differentiate between them by their function.

The Composite pattern has three main components. The base class that the other classes share is called the *Component*. This is the class with the common functionality for all classes. The *Leaf* is the object that makes up the individual objects that exist within the collection. The *Composite* is the class that forms the collection object itself. Both the leaf and the composite classes inherit from the component. This is done so that whether you call the individual leaf classes or the composite class, you still call the same method(s).

Suppose you wanted to make calls to a particular method on the class but, depending on whether the class was of type leaf or type composite, you wanted the method to work differently. If you called the method on a leaf, then you only executed the code in that leaf class. But, in the case of the composite class, when you call the method, the composite loops through all the leaf objects inside the composite and calls the method on each one. This allows you to use either a single object's method(s) or get a compounded effect for a whole collection of classes by calling all the leaf classes in the collection.

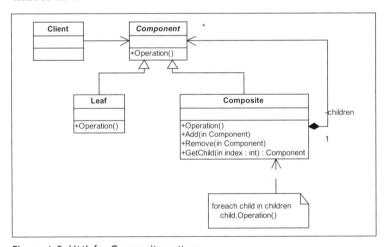

Figure 4-5. UML for Composite pattern

Problem: A way is needed to allow a group of classes with a common method and different functionality to work together in sequence without compiling the sequence beforehand

Our functional problem is a simple one. We start with a group of objects that each perform a different graphical function. We don't have a streamlined way to connect each one, but we need each object to be connected in a specific fashion and have each object call its Draw() method in the proper sequence.

```
//create all objects
OuterPanel root = new OuterPanel();
Circle circle = new Circle();
Square square = new Square();
Triangle triangle = new GraphicalComponent();
InnerPanel child = new InnerPanel();
Line line = new Line();

line.Draw();//first we need to draw the innermost object
child.Draw();//next the InnerPanel
//now we draw our remaining three graphical objects
circle.Draw();//Draw the circle object
square.Draw();//Draw the square object
triangle.Draw();//Draw the triangle object
root.Draw();//finally draw the outermost object
```

As you can see, this is not really very flexible. We have to make a lot of code changes to change the way the objects display. You may also notice there is no clear relationship between each object. So we may have trouble defining which object contains another object, and how the inner and outer objects affect each other. In other words, this is not a great model for object relationships. We see some of the classes appear to be named in such a way as to suggest they might be parents for other objects. This may be handled as hard coded inside each class's `Draw()` method, but is not intuitive based on the apparent class relationships.

In turn, we don't want to have to call the same method on each class over and over. We want the classes containing objects to be able to handle calls to their `Draw()` method, and also use the same method on each of their children.

Solution: Group each class into a composite, which will manage when each class will have its common method called and will allow manipulation of the sequence of calls

We have identified in our problem that we have a need for defining a relationship between parent and child classes. What we need is a way to encapsulate the child classes in parents, and have the parents responsible for how they interact with their children. We can assume each parent may have many children, so we will allow the parent objects to assume the role of a collection. It seems all the objects have a similar function, the `Draw()` method, so we will want a common base class for both the parent and child classes that defines this method.

The first step we will take is to define that base class. This base in the Composite pattern is the component. The component will have an abstract `Draw()` method, as well as any other needed methods, properties, or events to support the base class. We derive the common elements for the class from finding out each class's common elements and putting them into the base. For this case, since the `Component` class will be the base for the leaf collection objects, we will need to implement the basic equals implementation needed

Structural Patterns

for making indexing and comparisons in a collection object. We also want to have a private variable to capture the leaf object's name and a public property for this variable. We also add an abstract method, `Draw()`, which will be implemented in different ways in each of the inheriting subclasses.

```
//Component
abstract class Component
{
    private string _name;

    public Component(string name)
    {
        _name = name;
    }
    public string Name
    {
        get{return _name;}
    }
    public abstract void Draw();

    public override int GetHashCode()
    {
        return _name.GetHashCode ();
    }
    public override bool Equals(object obj)
    {
        if(obj != null && obj is Component)
            return _name.Equals (((Component)obj).Name);
        else
            return false;
    }
    public override string ToString()
    {
        return _name;
    }
}
```

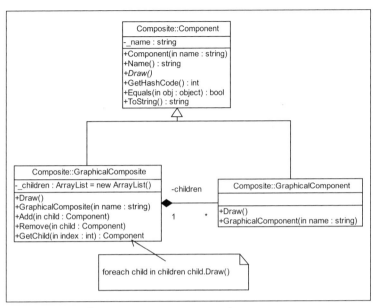

Figure 4-6. UML for Composite pattern example

Next we want to define our leaf class. Since this class will be our class for individual functionality, we will have the overridden `Draw()` method actually do something. In this case it will draw the graphical object:

```
//Leaf
class GraphicalComponent : Component
{
    public GraphicalComponent(string name) : base(name){}
    public override void Draw()
    {
        ......
    }
}
```

Lastly we create our composite object. The first thing we want to do is define a private collection variable to hold our leaf classes:

```
//composite
class GraphicalComposite : Component
{
    private ArrayList _children = new ArrayList();
```

We add a constructor, which takes the name of the component, along with methods to add and remove leaf objects from the collection:

```
public GraphicalComposite(string name) : base(name){}

public void Add(Component child)
{
    _children.Add(child);
}

public void Remove(Component child)
{
    _children.Remove(child);
}
```

We also add a way to feed an index into the collection and get back an individual leaf object. This might be useful if we just wanted to activate one object's Draw() method, instead of all of the objects contained in our composite.

```
public Component GetChild(int index)
{
    return (Component)_children[index];
}
```

And the last method we implement is our overridden Draw() method. Notice that this method has a looping algorithm to call each child leaf object's Draw() method in sequence. So if you call the parent class's method, then you also call all its childrens' methods for Draw() as well.

```
public override void Draw()
{
```

```
        foreach(Component comp in _children)
            comp.Draw();
    }
}
```

You are not limited to having leaf objects in your composite object. A composite class can also contain other composite classes, which also might hold a number of leaf classes. Although cardinality is not required by the pattern so that each parent and each child knows about itself, you could make this happen. In the basic case, you only have a one-sided relationship in that the composite always knows about its leaf objects, but the leaf objects do not know anything about their parent composite object.

When we now look at the implementation of our new Composite pattern, the first thing we notice is the apparent relationships that we create between our leaf and parent composite objects. When we add leaf classes to the outer composite object, this object actually contains them, establishing the parent-child relationship:

```
GraphicalComposite root = new GraphicalComposite("OuterPanel");
root.Add(new GraphicalComponent("Circle"));
root.Add(new GraphicalComponent("Square"));
root.Add(new GraphicalComponent("Triangle"));
```

We can also add another composite to our outermost one. As you see below, we create a second composite, add a leaf class, and then add the second composite to the first one. This provides a relationship down through the tree to all the leaves contained within the tree, including the ones contained in the other composites.

```
GraphicalComposite childComposite = new
        GraphicalComposite("InnerPanel");
childComposite.Add(new GraphicalComponent("Line"));
```

```
root.Add(childComposite);
```

As with any collection class, we can add and remove leaves and composites from any composite we wish. Since we defined the `Add()` and `Remove()` methods by a specific type (the `Component` class), to add or remove an object from the composite we only need to inherit from that type to add to the composite's underlying collection.

```
GraphicalComponent removable = new GraphicalComponent("Single Line");
root.Add(removable);
root.Remove(removable);
```

Now when we call the `Draw()` method on the outermost class, it in turn calls the same method for all the leaf objects contained within. It also calls the method on all the composites it may contain, which in turn will call their children, and so forth, until all classes in the tree have had their `Draw()` method called:

```
root.Draw();
------------
Test for Composite
Create Root 'OuterPanel' Composite..
Add 'Circle' to Root 'OuterPanel' Composite..
Add 'Square' to Root 'OuterPanel' Composite..
Add 'Triangle' to Root 'OuterPanel' Composite..

Create Child 'InnerPanel' Composite..
Add 'Line' to Child 'InnerPanel' Composite..
Add Child 'InnerPanel' to Root 'OuterPanel' Composite..
Add Child 'Single Line' Component to Root 'OuterPanel' Composite..

Remove Child 'Single Line' Component to Root 'OuterPanel' Composite..

OuterPanel.Draw() called to draw GraphicalComposite.
--Circle.Draw() called to draw GraphicalComponent.
--Square.Draw() called to draw GraphicalComponent.
```

```
--Triangle.Draw() called to draw GraphicalComponent.

InnerPanel.Draw() called to draw GraphicalComposite.
--Line.Draw() called to draw GraphicalComponent.
```

Comparison to Similar Patterns

As with any relational pattern, we have the ability to establish relationships between objects on a one-to-one or one-to-many basis. The Composite pattern has relationships to its other objects similar to many other relationship patterns. Just as the Chain of Responsibility can call each of its contained objects in turn, so can the Composite. The Composite pattern also can use one or all of the collection properties of the Iterator pattern, especially if you wish to control the rate of how your composite deals with each class in the collection. The Composite pattern is also similar to the Visitor and Flyweight patterns in that passed-in objects influence the overall Composite's behavior much as they do in both of these patterns. Decorators also have this effect, albeit the structure of a Decorator is much different than the Composite, and it is not a collection. We can use Decorators with the Composite pattern to provide another layer of flexibility to how the controls operate.

What We Have Learned

Using a Composite pattern is an intuitive way to define relationships between classes. It is useful in simplifying method calls when dealing with many objects in a collection. The pattern allows passed-in objects to modify overall behavior, giving a compounded effect for all the objects in the collection, as well as all underlying collections.

Related Patterns

- Chain of Responsibility pattern
- Command pattern
- Decorator pattern
- Flyweight pattern
- Iterator pattern
- Visitor pattern

Decorator Pattern

What Is a Decorator Pattern?

One of the most commonly used structural patterns used in GUI (graphical user interface) design is the *Decorator* pattern. The Decorator pattern gives us a way to use inheritance as a conditional add-on. What does this mean? It means that inheritance is used in the pattern in such a way as to make each inherited class be a sum of all the parts.

The Decorator pattern has four main parts: the *Component, Concrete Component, Decorator,* and *Concrete Decorator.* The component is usually an abstract class that holds the base functionality for both the non-decorated classes as well as the decorated ones. By non-decorated I mean without applying a decorator class to the existing component. The next aspect of the pattern is the concrete component. This is the non-decorated implementation class of the component, which we can instance without a decorator. The next part of the pattern gives us the name of the pattern. It consists of two parts: the decorator and the concrete decorator. The decorator is the abstract class that inherits from the component and holds an encapsulated instance of our desired concrete component. The concrete component is the implementation class with the added functionality desired for our decorator.

After reading the description above you may still be wondering how the pattern is useful. One use is to provide flexible inheritance. We can cast our decorator to be of the base type of component, which can give us all the same basic functionality we might have in a non-decorated control, but allows us to add desired functionality in an ad-hoc fashion. By making a control a decorator we add all the control's functions and a few desired new ones, or, if we wish not to have the new functionality, we can simply use the non-decorated control. This interchangeability gives us greater flexibility when dealing with inherited classes.

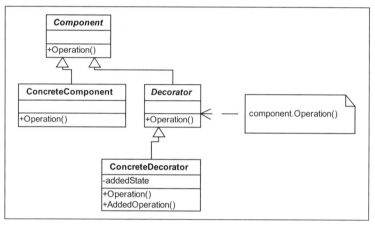

Figure 4-7. UML for Decorator pattern

Problem: We wish to have certain functions associated with a class type only when desired, but not all the time

Our functional problem involves a common user interface control inherited from an abstract base class. We would like at certain times to add functionality to the class, in this case scroll bar logic, but there are times when adding this logic is unwieldy or improper.

We start by looking at our abstract base class called
WindowControl. We notice that it contains a lot of
generic control sizing and positioning properties as we
might expect from a base graphical control. The control
also contains an abstract method called Render(), which
we can assume uses the other properties to make the control visible.

```
abstract class WindowControl
{
    private int _height;
    private int _width;
    private int _x;
    private int _y;

    public int Height
    {
        get{return _height;}
        set{_height = value;}
    }
    public int Width
    {
        get{return _width;}
        set{_width = value;}
    }
    public int XCoord
    {
        get{return _x;}
        set{_x = value;}
    }
    public int YCoord
    {
        get{return _y;}
        set{_y = value;}
    }

    public abstract void Render();
}
```

We already have this class in our code and it is functioning properly. We also want to take a look at the specific concrete implementation class to which we wish to add a decorator. The `TextBox` class inherits our abstract base and overrides the `Render()` method to perform the actual work of rendering the graphical aspects of the control. It takes in its constructor the properties necessary to perform this functionality. It also houses another instance variable, which does not have any effect on the rendering of the control.

```
class TextBox : WindowControl
{
    private string _value;

    public TextBox(int height, int width, int x, int y)
    {
        this.Height = height;
        this.Width = width;
        this.XCoord = x;
        this.YCoord = y;
    }

    public string Value
    {
        get{return _value;}
        set{_value = value;}
    }
    public override void Render()
    {
        Console.WriteLine("--TextBox Height:"+this.Height);
        Console.WriteLine("--TextBox Width:"+this.Width);
        Console.WriteLine("--TextBox X Coord:"+this.XCoord);
        Console.WriteLine("--TextBox Y Coord:"+this.YCoord);
        Console.WriteLine("--TextBox Value:"+_value);
    }
}
```

When we run the code it renders the `TextBox` class as expected. But there are times our text box needs some scroll bar logic added to it:

```
private int _scrollBarWidth;
private int _scrollBarPosition = 0;

public int ScrollBarWidth
{
    get{return _scrollBarWidth;}
    set{_scrollBarWidth = value;}
}
public int ScrollBarPosition
{
    get{return _scrollBarPosition;}
    set{_scrollBarPosition = value;}
}
```

We could just add this logic to the `TextBox` class, but it might be confusing or cause problems when using a non-scrollable text box. Also, because we don't want to render the scroll bar at all times with the text box, adding this functionality to the class would not be advisable. In short, it is not appropriate to add the scroll functions directly to the text box.

Another way we could accomplish this is to simply inherit from the `TextBox` class and create a scrollable `TextBox` class. This is not hard in simple implementations, but as complexity increases in the bases and across the inheritance chain, this can become problematic.

How do we confront this problem? Let's look at our solution section to see.

Solution: We allow a decorator that inherits from the class we are using to take its place and act as the class, but with the increased functionality of the decorator

When we look at our problem we easily could say we might add Boolean logic (if...then...else) to the render method to check the scroll values and render only if values were set:

```
public override void Render()
    {
        if(_scrollBarWidth > 0 && _scrollBarPosition > 0)
        {
        Console.WriteLine("--Scroll Bar Width:" + _scrollBarWidth);
        Console.WriteLine("--Scroll Bar Position:"
                        + _scrollBarPosition);
        }

        Console.WriteLine("--TextBox Height:"+this.Height);
        Console.WriteLine("--TextBox Width:"+this.Width);
        Console.WriteLine("--TextBox X Coord:"+this.XCoord);
        Console.WriteLine("--TextBox Y Coord:"+this.YCoord);
        Console.WriteLine("--TextBox Value:"+_value);
    }
```

But that would not really make use of OOP principles in our code or be intuitive when making changes. We can't quickly tell by this code whether or not we have a scrollable text box. We have to wait until run time and then try to see if valid values are present. This can be both confusing in the intent of the object as well as in violation of the rules of encapsulation: our class should only know about scroll bars if it really does have one.

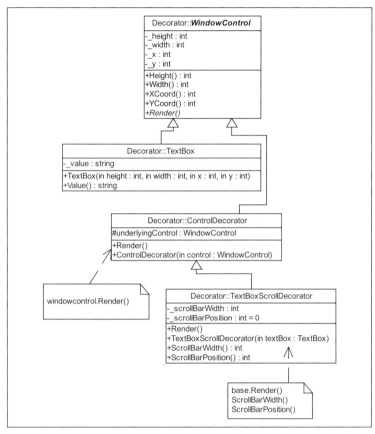

Figure 4-8. UML for Decorator pattern example

So we need another way to deal with this situation. A Decorator pattern seems to be the way to go. Using a decorator we can interchange our objects. We can use the decorated class when we need a scroll bar, and our `TextBox` class when we don't. Let's begin the refactoring effort at the point of creation of our decorator.

As we saw in our problem section, we already have the component and concrete component. For this refactoring effort, we don't wish to change either class. The true strength of the Decorator pattern comes to light in this. Since we don't have to modify existing functionality, we can easily start on the new aspects of code we wish to procure.

We start with our abstract decorator class. Following the pattern, we inherit this class from the abstract component we already have: WindowControl. We do this to provide the base functionality we might get with the TextBox class. Next, we need to provide a protected instance of our component. We do this so that a concrete instance can be passed and we can take advantage of that instance in our decorator. What we want is to capture all the functionality of our concrete component, while encapsulating it as an instance variable. Notice we also override the abstract method Render() and call our protected instance's Render() method inside. The instance is made protected so that the inherited concrete decorator can manipulate it directly.

```
abstract class ControlDecorator : WindowControl
{
    protected WindowControl underlyingControl;

    public ControlDecorator(WindowControl control)
    {
        underlyingControl = control;
    }
    public override void Render()
    {
        underlyingControl.Render();
    }
}
```

Next, we create our concrete decorator. This class is where we can directly add and change the functionality we get with our TextBox class. Generally, we want to add our new functionality of scroll bar logic to the existing

`TextBox` functionality. We inherit from the abstract base decorator class, and provide our instance variables for the scroll bar settings:

```
class TextBoxScrollDecorator : ControlDecorator
{
    private int _scrollBarWidth;
    private int _scrollBarPosition = 0;
```

The constructor for the class takes as its input parameter the `TextBox` object type. This is done to provide a more intuitive way to determine that we are decorating a `TextBox` class:

```
public TextBoxScrollDecorator(TextBox textBox) : base(textBox)
{
}
```

Next, we add our properties to set the scroll bar:

```
public int ScrollBarWidth
{
    get{return _scrollBarWidth;}
    set{_scrollBarWidth = value;}
}
public int ScrollBarPosition
{
    get{return _scrollBarPosition;}
    set{_scrollBarPosition = value;}
}
```

The last step is to override the `Render()` method and add our scroll bar rendering logic to it. Notice we call our base method first. We do this because in the rendering of the control to the user interface, the base text box component needs to be rendered before the scroll bar. This can be changed on a case-by-case basis.

Structural Patterns

```
public override void Render()
{
    base.Render();
    Console.WriteLine("Added decorator values:");
    Console.WriteLine("--Scroll Bar Width:" + _scrollBarWidth);
    Console.WriteLine("--Scroll Bar Position:"
                        + _scrollBarPosition);
}
}
```

Now we have all the necessary pieces to use our decorator. We need to look at how we can use the decorator and text box as interchangeable pieces. In our code we have need of a basic text box. We can instantiate this, set its properties, and call its Render() method:

```
TextBox textBox = new TextBox(250,350,1200,300);
textBox.Value = "Some Text...";
textBox.Render();
```

Next, in some other part of our code we need to make our text box scrollable. We need to use a type that inherits from the component, which our decorator does. We feed our previous text box instance to the decorator, set the scrollable components, and call its Render() method. The method on our decorator calls the encapsulated text box instance's method, and then adds its decorated render logic to it, giving a composite effect.

```
TextBoxScrollDecorator scrollable = new
        TextBoxScrollDecorator(textBox);
scrollable.ScrollBarPosition = 20;
scrollable.ScrollBarWidth = 10;
scrollable.Render();
```

The decorator implementation now gives us an intuitive and easily recognizable and interchangeable way to deal with adding functionality, without using direct chains of inheritance. We minimize confusion by decreasing the levels of inheritance between the `TextBox` class and any inherited classes we might otherwise create.

Comparison to Similar Patterns

The Decorator pattern is readily comparable with other patterns. One such pattern is the Adapter pattern. This pattern also hides another class's functionality within, and allows only an expected access to the inner class. Decorators often work well to increase the flexibility of Composites, where class relationships extend through a collection and methods can be called between several classes to create a composite whole.

What We Have Learned

Decorators give us a more flexible way to deal with class inheritance. They allow us to extend and interchange class types and functionality by allowing us to add new functionality to an existing class in a more easily recognizable and maintainable way. It gives us more explicit control of a class's functionality, without adding to the complexity of the code when using levels of inherited classes.

Related Patterns

- Adapter pattern
- Composite pattern
- Visitor pattern

Facade Pattern

What Is a Facade Pattern?

A *Facade* pattern allows grouping of subsystems behind a unified interface to allow a central access point to these subsystems. If you desired to limit the access to a group of subsystems or define a limited interface to these subsystems, you might use a facade. A facade is a way to control the access to these subsystems.

The Facade pattern has one main component: the *Facade Interface*. The facade interface may consist of several parts, but it is considered one component. This interface is the hub for accessing controlled subsystems inside an assembly or package.

There are many ways and reasons to use a facade. API layers are good examples of where and how to use a facade. An API layer allows certain functionality to be visible to code bases outside the API, but only allows specific interfaces to be used to access any code inside the API layer.

For instance, if you had a group of classes that together defined a particular code flow that made up a process, but calling these classes out of order would result in catastrophic failure of these subsystems, you could make all these classes internal to their assembly. This would hide these classes from access outside the assembly. You then could create a facade to encapsulate the calling order of each class, thereby controlling code flow behind the facade. By making each class internal to the assembly, you guarantee that you do not allow unexpected access to the classes. Inside the assembly you can decide when and where each class is called. Methods on the facade interface then could be provided to access the subsystem classes in a controlled fashion. No outside access to these classes would be permitted and only the code internal to the facade could decide the class's calling order, thus preventing a catastrophic failure. The facade could then allow controlled access to each class in its proper calling order, encapsulating the code flow of the entire subsystem structure.

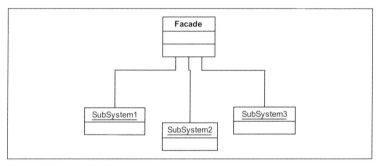

Figure 4-9. UML for Facade pattern

Problem: We have several classes whose methods make up a process, but we need to control the order in which these classes are called by code outside the assembly

For our functional example, we have a group of classes that reside inside an assembly that we want to make into an API (application program interface). Each class has functionality specific to a process flow, and together when called in the right order they produce the desired code implementation. But you have discovered that these classes are being called in code bases outside the one your API classes are in that cause a catastrophic failure in your API layer. You need some way to control how, when, and in which order each class is called. You also want to provide a simpler interface for code outside the assembly to call these classes. In short, you need a way to provide a single interface to access all the needed classes and their methods to accomplish a task.

```
...called from outside the API assembly

BusinessRules rules = new BusinessRules();
rules.GetRules();

BusinessDAL dal = new BusinessDAL();
dal.Update();

//calling the validation after the DAL update fails
BusinessValidation validation = new BusinessValidation();
validation.CheckIsValidRequest(updateValue);
```

Solution: Create a facade layer with interfaces to desired classes that are called in the proper order and allow the subsystem classes to only be called inside the facade assembly

Your solution is to provide a facade interface. The facade will allow you to control and limit the access to each subsystem class. It will also allow you to encapsulate the calling order or *order of operation* of the class group.

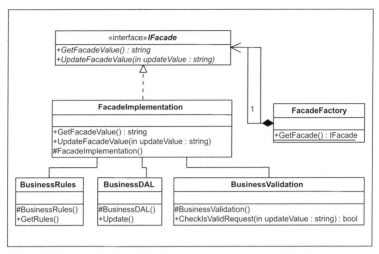

Figure 4-10. UML for Facade pattern example

The first step in implementing the Facade pattern is to make your subsystem classes inaccessible to any outside assembly. To do this in .NET you need to change the access modifier to `internal` for each class declaration. You also need to change the constructor to `protected internal` to guarantee that no access outside the current assembly is possible.

```
internal class BusinessDAL
{
    protected internal BusinessDAL(){}

    public void Update()
    {
        ...
    }
}

internal class BusinessRules
{
```

Structural Patterns

```
    protected internal BusinessRules(){}
    public void GetRules()
    {
        ...
    }
}

internal class BusinessValidation
{
    protected internal BusinessValidation(){}
    public bool CheckIsValidRequest(string updateValue)
    {
        ...
    }
}
```

Notice that each method above is public. Because the class is marked `internal`, the access to these methods is limited to instantiation of the class only inside the assembly or package. For Java implementations, you need not add any class access modifier; just declare the class thus:

```
class BusinessDAL {...}
```

This sets the access to internal to the package.

Now that you have all your subsystem classes in your assembly set to inaccessible, you need to build the external access interface you will use for the facade implementation:

```
public interface IFacade
{
    string GetFacadeValue();
    void UpdateFacadeValue(string updateValue);
}
```

For this example, we are allowing two methods to be accessed in the interface. These two methods will point back to our facade implementation class methods. The interface allows disconnected access outside the API layer.

Now we can create the implementation class that will house the facade functionality for each method. We create a class that implements the `IFacade` interface so we can have a place to implement our facade methods:

```
public class FacadeImplementation : IFacade
{
```

We set the constructor of our facade implementation class to `internal` in .NET. We do this in Java by using the keyword `protected`. This way we do not allow the facade to be created outside the assembly. Why would we do this? We want to allow access from outside our API layer to only the interface, not the implementation class of the facade. To do this, we need to limit the creation of the facade implementation class to a factory, which only returns the interface. In this way, we can guarantee that access outside our API layer is only done through the `IFacade` interface.

```
    protected internal FacadeImplementation()
    {

    }
```

Our implementation methods are all set to have public access modifiers. This is done to allow access to the facade methods outside the assembly or package.

```
    public string GetFacadeValue()
    {
        ...
    }

    public void UpdateFacadeValue(string updateValue)
    {
```

Structural Patterns

```
   ...
}
```

Now let's look at how we control the program flow of the subsystem classes inside the facade methods. For our example, we will look at the method that performs the update, which has several class methods that must be run in order to accomplish a task:

```
public void UpdateFacadeValue(string updateValue)
{
    BusinessValidation validation = new BusinessValidation();
    validation.CheckIsValidRequest(updateValue);
    BusinessRules rules = new BusinessRules();
    rules.GetRules();
    BusinessDAL dal = new BusinessDAL();
    dal.Update();
}
```

Notice each class is created and the order of operations is controlled in an expected fashion. Doing this accomplishes our goal of limiting access and allowing a controlled path through our subsystem code. Now when we call the facade interface from the factory we have a single route into the subsystem, and this route is determined inside the facade.

```
//Facade returned from factory.
IFacade facade = FacadeFactory.GetFacade();

// Facade subsystem update called:
facade.UpdateFacadeValue("some value");
--Validation subsystem called.
--Rules subsystem called.
--Data Access Layer subsystem called.
--Facade subsystems performed an update.
```

This makes it simpler for both the calling application, since it is given a simple access point, and the facade code, whose logical functional path is set and accessed in only one way.

Comparison to Similar Patterns

The Facade pattern is similar to the Proxy pattern in that they both provide access to subsystems. However, the Proxy pattern is better suited to remote access or multi-domain specific access, and the Facade is better suited to API or code layers within the same domain or code base. Adapters and Bridges could also be compared, but their functionality requires less abstraction of their subsystems than a facade suggests, requiring only some way for similar code bases to interact without sharing their underlying classes. Adapters and Bridges also require less structured and comprehensive restriction of the subsystems, usually only spanning the scope of specific classes, while a facade usually controls multiple classes and is always used to limit access to a package or assembly, controlling and defining the access and order of operations of these subsystem classes.

What We Have Learned

Facades are an interesting way to provide controlled access to classes within a package or assembly to code outside the assembly or package. It allows encapsulation of subsystem classes and provides a way to control the order of operations and interaction of these classes inside the assembly while providing a seamless access point outside the assembly.

Structural Patterns

Related Patterns

- Adapter pattern
- Bridge pattern
- Proxy pattern

Flyweight Pattern

What Is a Flyweight Pattern?

The *Flyweight* pattern allows you to support a large number of granular objects by allowing them to be shared with intrinsic values and stored within a factory. These shared objects can be modified by providing extrinsic values from their individual contexts. The fine-grained objects themselves do not need to know or have reference to the context at all as a rule.

The Flyweight pattern has three main components: the *Flyweight Factory*, the *Abstract Flyweight*, and the *Concrete Flyweight*. There is also the *Unshared Concrete Flyweight*. The flyweight factory acts as a repository for the shared flyweight classes and creates new ones if not already constructed. The abstract flyweight class defines the shared attributes common to any flyweight object of this type. It acts as an interface, which provides methods to receive the extrinsic state from a context. The concrete flyweight class defines and stores intrinsic state. It is shareable and its state must be independent of any context. The unshared concrete flyweight class defines flyweights that are not shared. It can have children that are shared, but since the flyweight interface only allows sharing and does not enforce it, this class is useful when a single unshared instance is required.

So what is a flyweight and what does it do? Well, imagine you had a program that required a large group of object instances to function. To create a different object for each instance would be very costly in regard to both CPU memory and program load. Therefore, instead of creating a

Structural Patterns

different object class for each instance, we allow shared objects that are independent of outside contexts. That is, we can share the objects repeatedly without allowing the intrinsic state to be modified.

Intrinsic state is the state that resides within the shared object and is independent of context. *Context* is the particular placement of each object in code flow, with the particular values and states associated with that context. The *extrinsic state*, or state that is associated with the context, is allowed to pass into the flyweight class without modifying the intrinsic state of the flyweight.

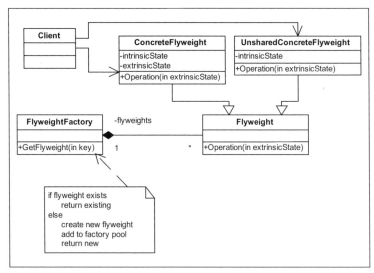

Figure 4-11. UML for Flyweight pattern

Problem: A text document uses individual object instances for each character and quickly becomes unwieldy

For our functional problem, we have a document program that has multiple character objects. These objects have gradually become unwieldy as we have added new characters to the document, and so we need a more efficient model to replace them. Right now, each character is represented by an object. When the user of the program adds another character to the document, it creates a new object and changes the font, size, and other attributes of the object and then adds this object to the document. As the user places more characters inside the document it starts to grow in size, making the program use an exponentially large amount of memory. Each character adds to the memory used by the document program. As the user types in more characters, the program starts to slow:

```
Document.AddCharacter(new Character('C',"Arial",8,"Black",140,100));
....... User types in 300 more characters
```

We need a way to allow each object to only be created once and, depending on its position in the document, have its state modified according to the formatting for that text section.

Structural Patterns

Solution: Use shared flyweight objects to instantiate a limited number of character objects that use their current context to change the extrinsic state

Our solution to the problem above is to use shared objects instead of creating new ones repeatedly. To accomplish this, we will create small granular objects called flyweights to hold only the basic definitions of a character. Since the characters we will use are used more than once inside our document object, we allow certain formatting to occur depending upon where in the document the character is placed. Each flyweight will have an intrinsic state that exists in the shared object, and methods to allow extrinsic state modification for each context that uses the shared object. The methods that allow extrinsic state to be modified will accept extrinsic state changes through the method's input parameters, but will not store them inside the object. So each call to these methods will only use the passed-in state values inside the method and will lose these values when the scope of the context has passed.

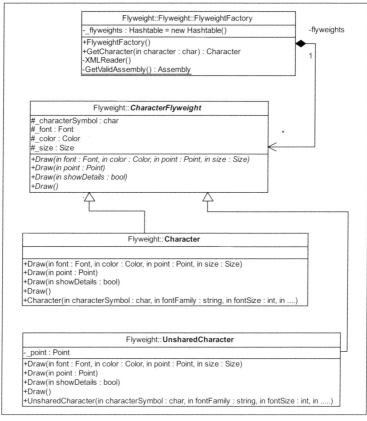

Figure 4-12. UML for Flyweight pattern example

The first step in implementing the pattern is capturing the variables that house the intrinsic state in our abstract flyweight object. We do this by providing them as protected variables accessible to their inherited classes:

```
abstract class CharacterFlyweight
{
    protected char _characterSymbol;
    protected System.Drawing.Font _font;
    protected System.Drawing.Color _color;
    protected System.Drawing.Size _size;
```

Next, we need to define the methods to allow the context to modify the extrinsic state. We use three methods overriding the base `Draw()` method that accept different state complexities. The number and type of methods are dependent on what you might actually need to modify in the extrinsic state inside the flyweight for the current context. Each method you use should allow different extrinsic state complexities to be modified from the default intrinsic state. The actual implementation of these methods should not, however, modify any intrinsic state variables.

```
public abstract void Draw(
    System.Drawing.Font font,
    System.Drawing.Color color,
    System.Drawing.Point point,
    System.Drawing.Size size);

public abstract void Draw(System.Drawing.Point point);
public abstract void Draw();
}
```

Next, we will create our concrete flyweight object. This is the actual shared implementation object. We define the input parameters for the constructor of the class to initialize the intrinsic state of the object. The object will be created in our factory object and the intrinsic shared state variables will be input by the factory upon class creation.

```
class Character : CharacterFlyweight
{
    public Character(
        char characterSymbol,
        string fontFamily,
        int fontSize,
        string color,
        int width,
        int height)
```

```
{
    _characterSymbol = characterSymbol;
    _font = new System.Drawing.Font(fontFamily, fontSize);
    _color = System.Drawing.Color.FromName(color);
    _size = new System.Drawing.Size(width, height);
}
```

We implement the abstract flyweight's extrinsic modification methods, allowing the passed-in state to override the intrinsic values only in the current context. These methods will be accessed by the context at run time and will change the way the character is rendered inside the document. The intrinsic values are not replaced or modified in this method because it would change the flyweight's intrinsic values throughout all contexts that are accessing this character throughout the document. Instead, depending on the complexity of state modification desired, the intrinsic values are replaced with the extrinsic ones during the execution of the Draw() method. Each method allows different complexities for state modification.

In this instance the method will change all state for the context of the method:

```
public override void Draw(
    System.Drawing.Font font,
    System.Drawing.Color color,
    System.Drawing.Point point,
    System.Drawing.Size size)
{
    .... All intrinsic state is replaced by the extrinsic
         state passed in
}
```

Structural Patterns

Here the method will replace only certain intrinsic values inside the method with extrinsic ones:

```
public override void Draw(System.Drawing.Point point)
{
    .... Only one intrinsic state value is replaced
}
```

And here the method allows the default intrinsic state to be used, passing in no extrinsic state changes to the method:

```
public override void Draw()
{
    .... Default intrinsic state is used unmodified
}
}
```

Next, we create our unshared flyweight. This class is very similar to the shared class except we require values that are associated directly with the context inside our constructor. We house these context-related values in a variable inside this class that stores the coordinates of the character within the document as a System.Drawing.Point object:

```
class UnsharedCharacter : CharacterFlyweight
{
    private System.Drawing.Point _point;

    public UnsharedCharacter(
        char characterSymbol,
        string fontFamily,
        int fontSize,
        string color,
        int width,
        int height,
        int xCoord,
        int yCoord)
    {
        _characterSymbol = characterSymbol;
```

```
        _font = new System.Drawing.Font(fontFamily, fontSize);
        _color = System.Drawing.Color.FromName(color);
        _size = new System.Drawing.Size(width, height);
        _point = new System.Drawing.Point(xCoord, yCoord);
    }
```

Inside the `Draw()` method we use the intrinsic `System.Drawing.Point` object to determine the placement within the document object. Since there is one unshared flyweight instance per context location, having intrinsic methods that associate with the context do not interfere with any other implementation of this object within the program.

```
public override void Draw(bool showDetails)
{
    Console.Write(String.Format("Intrinsic State: Font:{0},
                    Color:{1}, X/Y:{2}, Font Size:{3}, Symbol:{4}",
        new object[]{_font, _color, _point, _size, _characterSymbol}));
}
```

The last step in the pattern implementation is the flyweight factory. The factory will act as a creational construct for the individual shared flyweight classes. It will instantiate the class if not already created and store it for any context that wishes to access a flyweight. The factory has one main method called `GetCharacter`. This method returns a flyweight class creating the class if not already constructed. A hash table inside the factory acts as a storage repository, giving references to the shared flyweight objects to each context requesting an instance.

```
class FlyweightFactory
{
    private Hashtable _flyweights = new Hashtable();

    public Character GetCharacter(char character)
    {
```

```
        Character c = (Character)_flyweights[character];
        if(c == null)
        {
            XMLReader();
            c = (Character)_flyweights[character];
        }
        return c;
    }
    private void XMLReader()
    {
        ..... Creates characters identified in the xml config file
              and sets their intrinsic values...
    }

}
```

So now let's look at how the code works. First, we create an instance of our flyweight factory. Next, we call the `GetCharacter` method to retrieve a shared character flyweight object.

```
FlyweightFactory factory = new FlyweightFactory();
Character g = factory.GetCharacter('G');
```

Next, we call one of the extrinsic methods, passing in state variables telling the character object where in the document object to draw the point, what font to use, and so forth. This is what we mean when we say the context. The point in the code where we are when we make our extrinsic call to pass in the current context's values is the location of our current context.

```
g.Draw(new System.Drawing.Font("Georgia", 9),
    System.Drawing.Color.FromName("FloralWhite"),
    new System.Drawing.Point(200, 250),new
    System.Drawing.Size(45, 56));
```

If we look at the test output, we can see the extrinsic values are rendered in the document:

```
Extrinsic State: Font:[Font: Name=Georgia, Size=9, Units=3,
                       GdiCharSet=1, GdiVerticalFont=False],
                 Color:Color [FloralWhite], X/Y:{X=200,Y=250},
                 Font Size:{Width=45, Height=56}, Symbol:G
```

If we wanted to use the shared intrinsic state of the character, we could call the `Draw()` method with no parameters:

```
g.Draw();
```

In the last example above, since we did not modify the intrinsic context by calling the extrinsic method, the values should be the same for every call to the character object. If we looked at the intrinsic state in the test output, we would see that it had indeed not been modified by the previous extrinsic state method call of `Draw()`.

```
Intrinsic State: Font:[Font: Name=Microsoft Sans Serif, Size=9,
                       Units=3, GdiCharSet=1, GdiVerticalFont=False],
                 Color:Color [Black], Font Size:
                 {Width=140, Height=100}, Symbol:G
```

Next, we can call any other character as many times as we wish, setting the extrinsic state or allowing the default intrinsic state to be rendered to the document. We do not suffer a memory penalty in this way because we are reusing each character object repeatedly instead of creating a new character each time one is added to the document. We instead allow the document context to modify the character's position, font, color, and other variables, depending on where in the context we call each shared instance.

```
Character o = factory.GetCharacter('O');
o.Draw();
Character a = factory.GetCharacter('A');
a.Draw();
Character t = factory.GetCharacter('T');
t.Draw();
```

Lastly, let's look at the unshared concrete flyweight and talk briefly about its usage. As we stated above in our description of this object within the pattern, we do not have to have each flyweight object shared. The flyweight abstraction allows sharing, but no enforcement of sharing occurs. This is to allow unshared objects that may contain many shared flyweights as children. This gives us both the option of sharing objects or allowing many instances of objects to be created. This might be useful if we had a character that was only used rarely or needed special context-related conditions to be useful in the document, such as a paragraph element. For our example, we create an unshared flyweight object and pass in our context-related coordinates, font, size, color, and other relevant values:

```
UnsharedCharacter unshared = new
UnsharedCharacter('$', "Arial", 9, "Black", 140, 100, 223, 355);
```

Next, we call the intrinsic method `Draw()`. This method implementation will use our context-related data as passed into the constructor:

```
unshared.Draw();
------------
Test for Flyweight
Spell 'GOAT':
Extrinsic State: Font:[Font: Name=Georgia, Size=9, Units=3,
    GdiCharSet=1, GdiVerticalFont=False], Color:Color [FloralWhite],
    X/Y:{X=200,Y=250}, Font Size:{Width=45, Height=56}, Symbol:G

GOAT

Spell 'GAS':
Intrinsic State: Font:[Font: Name=Microsoft Sans Serif, Size=9,
    Units=3, GdiChar Set=1, GdiVerticalFont=False], Color:Color
    [Black], Font Size:{Width=140, Height=100}, Symbol:G
```

```
GAS

Get Unshared Character:
$
```

The particular context of the unshared character object gives us back the intrinsic values from that context.

Comparison to Similar Patterns

The Flyweight pattern uses both the State and Factory patterns to allow its implementation to work. This is one of the better examples of using a factory to manage shared objects, maintaining their state across context calls. This pattern would work well with the Composite pattern to identify parent to child hierarchical relationships inside the document. This kind of tree relationship would also help to group objects for the context. For example, you might use the Composite pattern to house groups of characters to share similar fonts or other attributes. This pattern also resembles the Strategy pattern in that the flyweights are small strategy classes handled by the flyweight factory. Each flyweight, depending on context, could be identified as a separate algorithm and each is interchangeable.

What We Have Learned

Flyweights allow us to control program size and keep it from becoming unmanageable. They allow us to share object instances instead of creating new objects for programs containing very granular and numerous objects. Using a shared or unshared interface, we can allow the current code flow to change the extrinsic attributes related to the flyweights without modifying the intrinsic shared attributes, thereby allowing context changes on objects to occur instead of facilitating the need for unnecessary object creation. This pattern usually works well if numerous object instances would slow down the system and allowing shared relationships for the context of the program to operate against would be possible.

Related Patterns

- Composite pattern
- Factory pattern
- Interpreter pattern
- State pattern
- Strategy pattern
- Template pattern

Proxy Pattern

What Is a Proxy Pattern?

Proxies generally provide a stub or placeholder for an actual implementation object. It allows the creation, security, or accessibility to be handled outside the current code domain, or latently handled on another address space. There are generally thought to be four main types of proxies:

- A *Remote Proxy* provides a localized stub, placeholder, or interface for an object in a different address space. If you had a program on a different server or on a different domain to which you wished to provide a controlled reference, this type of proxy might come into use.

- A *Virtual Proxy* only creates objects when asked. In other words, if you have an interface to this kind of proxy, it may only create the actual object the interface references when you actually make a method call or direct reference to the item.

- A *Protection Proxy* controls security to the actual object the proxy references. You might use this when an object has different security accessibility than the domain or address of where the proxy might be referenced. Depending on the access point or the level of security from the accessing program, this proxy might allow or fail a call to its referenced object.

- A *Smart Reference* or *Smart Pointer* handles object referencing of the actual object the proxy represents. It can monitor the number of threads accessing the actual object and free resources when necessary. It can load the persistent object into memory when referenced and handle initialization. It can handle transactional locking on the actual object so that other calls to that object cannot change the object while locked.

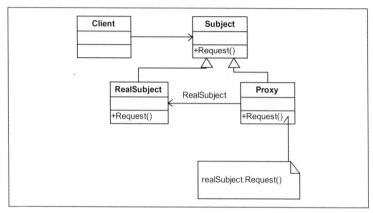

Figure 4-13. UML for Proxy pattern

The Proxy pattern has three main components: the *Subject*, the *RealSubject*, and the *Proxy*. The subject defines the common interface for the real subject and proxy. The real subject is the actual object that the proxy represents. The proxy maintains the reference to the real subject and acts as the access point for the real subject.

The most common usage for a proxy is when you have two incompatible systems or two separate domains and wish to allow these systems or domains to have access points to each other. Another common use for a proxy is to control access to an object to programs outside its domain or address space. Inside the proxy you can manage the access to external domains to any object you desire. The proxy can initialize the actual object and check the security level of the calling program. It can manage multiple instances of the objects or handle the unit of work for the object from outside access points.

Problem: You have an object in a different domain or server address you would like to access in the current domain, but do not want to allow construction of the object in the local domain

For our example, we need to create a way to access a program that can run in its own domain space. It would be too costly to run the program in the current domain space, or the program we wish to run simply resides in another domain space for security reasons. We need to access the program but do not want to load it right away. Currently we create the objects in our current domain. However, we might want several other application domains to access the object, and do not wish each domain to create instances of the object in an unmanaged fashion. We also wish to have a central point for managing instances and security for the actual object's domain. Below, we see the code in our current domain:

```
Subject subject = new Subject();
return subject.GetRequest();
```

For the reasons above we wish to provide a central access point for the `Subject` object's `GetRequest()` method. We wish to hide and encapsulate the security protocols, initialization, and instance creation of the `Subject` object. In addition, we need a way to share desired functionality either remotely or between otherwise incompatible domains.

Structural Patterns

Solution: Use a proxy to bridge the two separate domains and allow access between programs

We will allow a multitude of different domains to access our proxy object. The proxy object will handle how and when we create our `Subject` object implementation. It will also mask any initialization and the pointer into the domain where the `Subject` object exists.

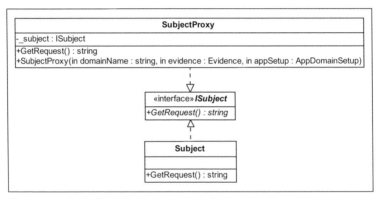

Figure 4-14. UML for Proxy pattern example

The first step in building a proxy around our `Subject` object is to refactor our existing `Subject` object and create the `ISubject` interface. This interface works to define the functionality shared between the `Subject` and `Proxy`:

```
// Subject
public interface ISubject
{
    string GetRequest();
}
```

Next, we refactor our `Subject` object and implement the `ISubject` interface. Notice the `GetRequest()` method carries over in this object and has no changes:

```
// RealSubject
class Subject : MarshalByRefObject, ISubject
{
    public string GetRequest(){ return "Request Found"; }
}
```

Next we create the `Proxy`. The proxy for this example creates a new application domain and initializes the `ISubject` interface inside this new domain. For a more realistic implementation we could allow the proxy creation to supply the intended domain name and details for security and setting up the new domain code base:

```
// Remote Proxy Object
class SubjectProxy : ISubject
{
    private ISubject _subject;

    public SubjectProxy(
        string domainName,
        System.Security.Policy.Evidence evidence,
        System.AppDomainSetup appSetup)
    {
        AppDomain domain = System.AppDomain.CreateDomain(
            domainName, evidence, appSetup);
        //creates a {System.Runtime.Remoting.
                    Proxies._TransparentProxy}
        //proxy stub to Examples.Proxy.Subject
        _subject = (ISubject)domain.CreateInstanceAndUnwrap(
            "Examples", "Examples.Proxy.Subject");
    }
}
```

Our proxy accesses the `GetRequest()` method on the `Subject` object and returns the result. Notice we are using the proxy stub to the `ISubject` interface created in the new application domain:

Structural Patterns

```
public string GetRequest()
{
    return _subject.GetRequest();
}
```

So if we wanted to call this proxy code in another domain, all we need to do is specify the domain details:

```
AppDomainSetup setup = new AppDomainSetup();
setup.ApplicationBase = path;
setup.ConfigurationFile = "(some file)";
```

And the security details that were needed to access our proxy:

```
// Set up the Evidence
Evidence baseEvidence = AppDomain.CurrentDomain.Evidence;
Evidence evidence = new Evidence(baseEvidence);
evidence.AddAssembly("(some assembly)");
evidence.AddHost("(some host)");
```

We pass these details into our proxy to identify the new domain, and call the GetRequest() method:

```
SubjectProxy proxy = new SubjectProxy("SubjectDomain",
                                     evidence, setup);
return proxy.GetRequest();
```

When we look at the code at run time, we can see where the new domain occurred that is accessing our proxy and see that our proxy passed the value from the GetRequest() method back into this domain:

```
using remoting.....System.Runtime.Remoting
Domain {SubjectDomain} created in:
C:\projects\DesignPatternsBook\src\Examples\bin\
Cross Domain Proxy results:Request Found
```

Comparison to Similar Patterns

Proxies give us another way to join code that exists in incompatible objects and domains. It works much like the Adapter pattern, in that it hides the subject behind an interface and only allows controlled access to the objects that make up the subject. Bridges offer similar functionality. The Facade pattern is more like the proxy than these other two in that it hides a group or subsystem of objects. The difference in the Proxy pattern is it is designed to work with a little more separation of platforms, and handles object creation, security, and cleanup in a separate domain context.

What We Have Learned

Proxies allow us to maintain true separation of code from a point of view of ownership and control of underlying classes that the proxy provides access to. All access that a proxy controls should be handled by the proxy as a separate domain; in other words, the process flow model performs its operations separately from the executing call.

Related Patterns

- Adapter pattern
- Bridge pattern
- Facade pattern

Glossary of Terms

This glossary contains terminology definitions as they fit into this book. These definitions are not meant to be used outside of the context of the book or chapters where the term is used.

abstraction: Refers to the way objects allow subclassing and polymorphic instances of themselves to manifest, keeping core functionality and allowing these instances to change this functionality based on their context and usage needs.

bitwise: Working with data on the byte level. A bitwise comparison compares a series of single bytes or a pair of bytes to see if they are equal in binary fashion. Bitwise operators work with the bytes of data rather than their values.

clone: An instanced copy of an object and its properties and intrinsic values.

configuration file: A resource file for application configuration, usually static to the run-time application and used to initialize or configure global application resources.

context: The particular placement of each object in code flow, with the particular values and states associated with that context.

contract: A way to refer to code interfaces and abstractions; a definition of code that shares similar interfaces.

deep copy: A complete copy of the entire class encapsulation including all collections and variables, making the object independent in regard to the object from which it was cloned.

dirty updates: Refers to a unit of work when two different workflows consecutively update the same record; in effect, the last consecutive workflow cancels out the updates performed by the other workflows. This usually happens when two users update the same record without being forced to retrieve current data before the update.

encapsulation: Basic object-oriented methodology rule that allows different visibility of attributes and methods depending on their access level. Access to different levels of code and objects is set and used at compile time to create access rules around these entities.

enum: A .NET construct for a value type that supplies names for underlying primitive types.

getter: A property accessor, specific to .NET, that allows access to a private variable in a controlled fashion.

implementation: The act of creating a non-abstracted object. This is the actual object from which instances are created during run time. This would signify any non-abstract class.

inheritance: Basic object-oriented methodology rule that allows objects to be derived from other objects. These derived objects will contain, based on the access level, all the features of the parent object, but allow polymorphism of methods and attributes as allowed by the parent.

interface: Any construct or definition that allows objects with no similar linkages to connect and communicate.

lazy load: A way to defer the actual full creation and instantiation of a class to when it is actually needed. A class can be created but not fully configured until a call to an instance is made. This method allows objects with a high cost of creation to defer some of the creational aspects to occur over time instead of all at once.

lock: The `lock` keyword from .NET is used to keep multiple threads from accessing the code at the same time. It keeps the access to the code block concurrent and synchronized. This is how we only create one object instead of allowing each thread in turn to create another instance of the object. Java uses the `synchronized` keyword to perform the same functionality.

MDI (multiple document interface): Any windows forms application that uses parent and child forms with the child forms being contained inside the parent's borders and domain.

metadata: Any language data (like XML schemas) that is used by a computational system to determine functionality by interpreting this data. Used in workflow systems where logic is not compiled directly into immutable executables, but instead is kept in an editable form and sent to the executable code to be interpreted and used to determine the logical workflow at run time.

mutex: A thread synchronization object that allows only one thread at a time to access a resource.

order of operation: The order during run time in which objects interact in a particular thread.

polymorphism: Basic object-oriented methodology rule that allows objects that share a common bond to be changed depending on their state, level of inheritance, or context. Each object can be changed or morphed, depending on its usage, from a common object or object definition. For example, a base object has a method that returns a value. This method also exists in its children, but the return value is slightly different from the parent depending on the child object type.

refactoring: This principle is one of continuous improvement. You make small changes over time to code, which leads to improvements in the overall code. You avoid large changes, preferring small changes that can create an overall effect of better, more maintainable, scaleable, and portable code. When a large change is indicated, this is no longer refactoring but is redesigning, and should be treated with the appropriate impact to your project this implies. So it is in the best interest of the developer to make sure refactoring efforts do not extend in scope to redesign.

reflection: In modern software programming, to look at the code structure of classes' assemblies and objects, and analyze that structure during run time.

repositories: Any classes that contain other classes or collections of classes.

semaphore: A thread synchronization object that acts as a gate and allows only a set number of threads to access a resource.

shallow copy: An object that may share data with the original copy.

state: The intrinsic and extrinsic values of a class or object at run time.

static: An object or method that can be shared between different threads. Each thread can access a static method or object at any time and there is no guaranteed concurrency between these threads.

subclassing: Deals with abstraction and inheritance. The ability to create classes based on or derived from parent classes, in order to share or limit functionality.

synchronized: This Java keyword is used to keep multiple threads from accessing the code at the same time by allowing each thread to access the code inside the keyword block in sequential turns.

unit of work: A series of tasks that together complete a cycle. This refers to how a workflow accomplishes a series of tasks inside a transaction or context. Each particular function contributes and is associated with some part of a unit of work if each function depends on the other to complete a task.

virtual: Refers to objects and schemas as non-actual or unrelated to actual objects or schemas. Virtual also refers to abstraction in class children. A virtual method would be one that is non-abstract but marked for override in derived child classes.

Index

contract, 51
creational methods, defining, 49-55
creational patterns, 17
   abstract factory pattern, 41-56
   builder pattern, 57-73
   factory pattern, 18-40
   prototype pattern, 74-80
   singleton pattern, 81-89

D
database transactions, encapsulating, 195-202
date formats, managing, 109-113
decorator pattern, 235-236
   related patterns, 245
   using, 236-245
deep copy, 78
design patterns, 1
   cross-referencing, 14
dirty updates, 164, 167
domains, bridging, 271-274

E
encapsulation, 2-4
equals implementation, 10, 12
   testing, 13
extrinsic state, 256

F
facade pattern, 246-247
   related patterns, 253-254
   using, 247-253
factories, 18
   abstract, *see* abstract factories
factory pattern, 18-20
   related patterns, 39-40
   using, 21-39
flyweight pattern, 255-256
   related patterns, 267-268
   using, 257-267
functionality, sharing, 185-191

G
Gang of Four, 17

H
hashing algorithm, ensuring unique, 11

I
inexact match, 216-217
inheritance, 9-10
   using to identify class types, 35-39
instance, maintaining, 82-88
interface, 5
interpreter pattern, 108-109
   related patterns, 118-119
   using, 109-118
intrinsic state, 256
iterator pattern, 120
   related patterns, 127
   using, 121-126
iterators, 120

K
keywords
   lock, 85, 170
   synchronized, 85

L
lazy loading, 28
list, moving through elements in, 121-126
lock keyword, 85, 170
logic, encapsulating, 21-24

M
mediator pattern, 128-129
   related patterns, 135
   using, 129-135
memento pattern, 136-137
   related patterns, 144
   using, 137-143

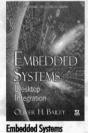

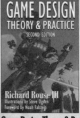